TO ENJOY HIM

FOREVER

by

Malcolm Webber

PIONEER BOOKS

Published by:

Pioneer Books
58896 Timber Trail
Goshen, Indiana 46526-8614
U.S.A.

(219) 533-9774

Please write for more information.

All Scripture references are from the King James Version of the Bible, unless otherwise noted.

Printed in the United States of America.

ISBN: 0-9626908-0-5

CONTENTS

I am Yours, and You are mine;
Let there come nothing between us.
Let my life be one with Thine;
Eternally hid in Your Presence.

Nothing more than Thee I desire;
To know Thee fully in my heart.
My soul's design to go with Thee higher,
And be found, my life hid with Christ in God.

TO ENJOY HIM FOREVER

The Westminster Assembly convening at Edinburgh, July 2, 1648, approved the "Larger Catechism", the first question of which asks, "What is the chief and highest end of man?" In reply, the answer is given, "Man's chief and highest end is to glorify God, and fully to enjoy Him for ever."

In a former volume we have touched upon the glory of God as the final and ultimate end of all things. In this present volume we will seek to introduce the subject of the enjoyment of God in His creation and His man's enjoyment of Him.

All we can do is begin the subject. Only each of us personally can continue it.

As we commit this book to print, our prayer is that it will be effective as another of the many voices in this critical hour calling Jesus' bride to the simplicity that is in Himself.

Malcolm Webber
Kimmell, Indiana
March, 1990

O Jesus, King most wonderful,
Thou Conqueror renowned,
Thou Sweetness most ineffable,
In whom all joys are found!

When once Thou visitest the heart,
Then truth begins to shine,
Then earthly vanities depart,
Then kindles love divine.

O Jesus, Light of all below!
Thou Fount of life and fire!
Surpassing all the joys we know,
And all we can desire,—

May every heart confess Thy Name,
And ever Thee adore,
And, seeking Thee, itself inflame
To seek Thee more and more.

Thee may our tongues for ever bless,
Thee may we love alone,
And ever in our lives express
The image of Thine own.

(Bernard of Clairvaux)

CHAPTER ONE

God's Eternal Purpose is Fellowship

*And the LORD God said, It is not good that the
man should be alone; I will make him a helper suited
to him. (Gen. 2:18, Hebrew)*

In the beginning, after God had created man, He looked
upon him and saw that man needed a "helper". But not just
any helper would do. This had to be a "helper suited to
him". God created all the animals and brought them to
Adam, but there was not found a suitable companion for
him. So then God created a woman to be his companion.
And He did not create her out of the ground as the animals
had been, but He took a part of Adam and made her **out of
him**.

Because woman now partook of man she became a
suitable companion for him. She was of his nature: "bone
of my bones, and flesh of my flesh". Nothing less than this
could have satisfied man. Adam's companion had to be like
him, of his nature, of his image, or else the companion
could never have satisfied him. In order for there to be a
lasting and fulfilling relationship between man and his
companion, she had to be made out of him.

That this fellowship between a husband and his wife
is a Divinely-intended type of the relationship between
Jesus and His bride is expressed in Paul's letter to the
saints at Ephesus:

*For no man ever yet hated his own flesh; but
nourisheth and cherisheth it, **even as the Lord the
church:***

9

For we are members of His body, of His flesh, and of His bones.

For this cause shall a man leave his father and mother, and shall be joined unto his wife, and they two shall be one flesh.

*This is a great mystery: but **I speak concerning Christ and the church**. (Eph. 5:29-32)*

In the Garden of Eden, God could undoubtedly have created His man to have been an "island" in himself. He could have created him to have not even needed a companion. To do this would have been possible for God, but it was not His purpose. Similarly, the Son of God does not need a man to fellowship with nor to make Himself complete;[1] but He chose to make His man in His image[2] not only to make communion **possible** between His man and Himself, but so that this communion would truly be **pleasing** to God as well as to man.

We repeat, the reason God made man in His image was so that He could fellowship and commune with him, in such a way that was actually pleasing and enjoyable to Himself.

This is beautifully reflected in the husband-wife relationship. The reason a man marries a wife is not just for her benefit—so that she will have a provider and protector—but he also marries her for his own benefit. And his benefit consists in more than just having someone to cook, clean and care for him. A large part of the reason for him marrying is his need for companionship.

From the union of husband and wife, something is born that goes beyond the mutual utility of the

---

1. In the eternal fellowship of the triune Godhead, God has always been **complete** and **content** in Himself.

2. Gen. 1:26; 2:7; 5:1; 9:6; 1 Cor. 11:7; Jam. 3:9

arrangement. There is something far deeper involved than the mere formality of two individuals living together for the superficial helping of each other. There is a spiritual union and bond that comes to pass between the two: "and they two shall become one flesh". There comes about an intangible relationship between them which satisfies not just their physical needs but also their emotional and spiritual needs for companionship.

By "companionship" we mean more than just physical proximity and communication. We mean the deepest possible realization of an inner fellowship—a spiritual union and bond—an experience of true love.

Whether or not this fellowship is ever realized in many marriages does not change the fact that this was God's principal intention in establishing the marriage relationship. Indeed this was His very purpose in creating woman in the beginning: so that Adam could become "one flesh" with her.

This deep fellowship is what Paul refers to in his letter to the Ephesians, when he speaks of the husband-wife relationship; and it is this context in which he writes, "I speak concerning Christ and the church", thereby showing that the relationship of a man to his wife is an intended type or picture of the relationship between Christ and His church. This is also stated in Paul's first letter to the Corinthian church:

> ... for two, saith He, shall be one flesh. But he
> that is joined unto the Lord is one spirit (i.e. with
> Him). (1 Cor. 6:16-17)

So we see that when God created man He had a deeper purpose in mind than merely to create a world and then someone to rule over it on His behalf. If this was all He wanted, He could have simply created a being who was not in His image but who was superior enough to the rest

11

of the created order to exercise dominion over it all in His place. But this was not God's highest purpose. He had a greater purpose than dominion and it is revealed in the fact that He created man **in His own image**.

Just as Eve had to be made in the image of Adam—actually out of Adam—in order for a true fellowship of love to be possible between her and Adam, so man had to be created in the image of God—actually from the breath of God—in order for an intimate relationship of love to be possible between God and His man. God's purpose in the creation of man was fellowship: fellowship with Himself. This was in His heart from the very beginning.

This purpose has never changed. Although Adam sinned and plunged himself and his descendants into a state of alienation from their Creator, God graciously provided for the redemption of His man—to open for His man a way back to Himself. Again His purpose was not mere utility. Jesus did not die upon the cross simply to legally remit man's sins, and deliver him from his well-deserved punishments, both temporal and eternal. Neither did He die just to demonstrate His own infinitely glorious attributes of grace, love and mercy. Of course the death of Christ did accomplish all this; indeed if it had only accomplished these things it would have been a work of infinite glory. But, amazingly, a central purpose of God in the shedding of the blood of His Son was to reconcile man to Himself: to restore the lost fellowship. "Christ ... once suffered for sins ... **that He might bring us to God**".[1]

So we see that we have been redeemed unto fellowship with God. The purpose of our redemption was not simply to deliver us from eternal hell, but God desires fellowship and communion with His man. This is the essence of

---

1. 1 Pet. 3:18; 2 Cor. 5:18

salvation and it is stated in many ways in the New Testament, where it is said that:

we have been reconciled to God;
we now have peace with God;
we are accepted in the beloved;
we are received by God;
we are to abide in Him, and He in us;
we are partakers of the Divine Nature;
we are now alive unto God;
we are born of God;
we are children of God;
we are heirs of God;
we are the bride of Christ;
we now have access unto the Father;
we are made nigh to God;
Jesus is not ashamed to call us brethren;
Jesus now calls us his friends.

All of these are profound statements, and they are all **concrete** statements, reflecting **concrete** truths.

We must not reduce our salvation to a mere theory of legal standing! These scriptures mean more than that. It is unbelief and mysticism to devalue the Christian life to mere ideas about theoretical position. Certainly we do now have a glorious legal standing with God. But the above statements from the New Testament are not only legal truths—they are intended to be **experiential** ones as well. In fact that is their **primary** meaning. **Jesus now calls us His friends!** This is not religious speculation nor some theological construct to be discussed and debated—this is an experience to be lived!

Friends of God

Adam enjoyed a real fellowship with God before his sin disrupted the relationship. He did not conjecture nor philosophize about God; **he walked with God** in the cool of the evening. Adam knew God; he talked to God; he enjoyed God; and he returned a fellowship back to God that God Himself actually enjoyed.

Adam was not just a servant, a subordinate slave to God; he was God's **friend!**

In the beginning, before God created woman for man, He created all the animals; but among them there was not found "a helper suited to him (i.e. man)". Animals can **serve** man, but they are not able to **fellowship** with him nor to return love to him. The only communication possible is at best only superficial and limited. This limitation is because of the difference in natures. Animals were not created out of man but out of the ground.[1] There is no true union nor communion possible.

This, however, is not the case between man and his wife. Because woman participates in man's nature, there is possible a mutually pleasing and fulfilling relationship between the two. The creation of woman filled a need, not for a servant, but for an intimate fellow.

And it is so between man and his God, in which instance there has been a partaking of nature in three ways. Firstly, man originally partook of the Divine nature when he was created in the image and likeness of God, literally by the breath of God.

Secondly, God partook of the nature of man when the eternal Son was made flesh and dwelt among us; being born of a woman and living upon this earth; tempted in all points like as we are; suffering real sufferings;

---

1. Gen. 1:24; 2:19

14

experiencing real hunger, thirst and tiredness. Jesus is truly and forever a man: spirit, soul, mind and body.

Lastly, man again receives of God's nature when the Creator by His grace breathes once more into the nostrils of man His own Divine life in the new birth, implanting His incorruptible Seed of life within us. In fulfillment of the eternal purposes of God, we have become "bone of His bones, and flesh of His flesh"—"one spirit with the Lord". So it is possible for there to be fellowship between God and man, and even more than fellowship—**a union**.

The miracle is not that God, from His side, can talk to man, just as it is no great thing that man can talk to animals. The miracle is that (unlike in the relationship of animals to man) man can not only understand his God, but he can respond to Him in a way that is genuinely pleasing to God. Consider how marvelous it would be if this were the ability of animals toward man. That this reciprocal communication is possible between God and man is vastly more marvelous, considering the infinite person and grandeur of God. Remember that this is only possible due to the community of nature between God and man.

So we see that God's purpose in creating man was so there could be a genuine relationship and mutually fulfilling fellowship between Himself and man.

God's Original Purpose Will be Fulfilled

When Adam sinned, the relationship was destroyed. But Christ went to the cross to make a way back for man to God; and in so doing He opened once more the door to fellowship, to intimate relationship. This is what the Christian life is—**restoration to fellowship with our Creator**—it is nothing less. We have been restored, not just to a legal standing, but to a living vital experience. God has apprehended us that we, in turn, should apprehend

15

Him. He has chosen once again to know man, that man should once again know Him.

The Lord Himself declared in the Prophets that a fundamental purpose of the New Covenant would be that "they shall all **know** me, from the least of them unto the greatest of them."[1] And again, it is written by the Apostle John:

*And we know that the Son of God is come ... **that** **we may know Him** that is true (1 John 5:20)*

The Christian life **is** the restoration of man to fellowship with God—it means nothing less.

*And this **is** life eternal, **that they might know thee** the only true God, and Jesus Christ, whom thou hast sent. (John 17:3)*

We are called, not just to live forever in heaven, but to walk with God, to experience God, to know God, to talk to God, to love God, to enjoy God, and to return a fellowship back to God (incredible as it sounds!) that God Himself actually enjoys.

---

1. Jer. 31:33-34; see also 1 John 2:20, 27; cf. Ps. 68:18; Song of Sol. 4:9-5:1; 7:6, 10; Ps. 147:11; 149:4a

CHAPTER TWO

The Entrance To Fellowship is Christ's Cross

And they heard the voice of the LORD God walking in the garden in the cool of the day: and Adam and his wife hid themselves from the Presence of the LORD God amongst the trees of the garden ...

So He drove out the man; and He placed at the east of the garden of Eden Cherubim, and a flaming sword which turned every way, to keep the way of the tree of life. (Gen. 3:8, 24)

When Adam sinned, he became alienated from God. Through his disobedience to God, he lost not just the Garden of Eden, and not just his physical life, and not just earthly prosperity, blessing and provision. He lost something far greater than all that. He lost **God**.

God had warned man that if he ate of the fruit of the tree of knowledge of good and evil, he would die in the same day. And when Adam and Eve rebelled and ate, they died—and the whole human race died in them. All men came under the curse of death, both physically and spiritually.

From that time forward men's bodies began to die, heading irrevocably towards final physical demise and corruption. All men were henceforth born literally in a state of death from the time of conception. From the day of Adam's sin man's health began to degenerate, he becoming subject to a seemingly infinite variety of sicknesses and diseases. From the time of Adam's sin, he would no longer happily dress and keep the Garden of his provision, but all his necessary sustenance would be

17

brought forth by "the sweat of his face". From that time forward man would no longer live in harmony with nature, but it would seem that God's entire created order was ruthlessly bent on annihilating him with all his civilization and all the work of his hands. Neither would man, from that time forward, ever again live in harmony with himself. The earth soon tasted of the blood of murder,[1] a firstfruits of the vast violence, torture, strife and war that would quickly fill the world. All these things Adam lost when he sinned. Yet they were not all he lost, neither were they the worst of his loss. But man lost something far greater than all these things. **He lost God.**

Gone were the days of communion with God, in the cool of the evening when man and his Creator would walk and talk together. Gone was the fellowship that finite man once enjoyed with infinite God. Adam was now cast out of the Garden, prevented from ever returning by Cherubic guards and a whirling, flaming sword.

Moreover, denied access to physical proximity to God was not all that the dissolution of their relationship consisted in. In the day that Adam ate of the fruit, man died inwardly and spiritually. He died to God. He died to the Presence of God. That precious, beautiful, sweet Presence that once he knew and lovingly delighted in, man now fled and hid himself from.

Tragedy of tragedies! Gone **forever**, was that blessed fellowship, the crowning glory of God's created order—man, in God's own image, marvelously able to commune with his Maker in a manner not only pleasing to himself, but also to the Infinite One. Now that precious fellowship was gone—**gone forever!**[2]

---

1. Gen. 4
2. But for the gracious provision of God, of course.

18

Even as the fulfillment of the original relationship was mutual, so now the breakdown of the relationship was also from both sides. Man was forthwith incapable of fellowship with God. Corrupted and depraved from the depths of his being, **dead** to God, **alienated** from God, man no longer sought God. In fact he now **refused** to know Him, and hid from Him, disdainfully commanding Him, "Depart from us; for we desire not the knowledge of thy ways". No longer able to love his Creator, man became an "enemy" and a "hater" of God.[1]

By necessity, although not without reluctance, God forced man from His Presence. Being of "purer eyes than to behold evil", and by nature unable to countenance iniquity, God drove His man from Him. The relationship was ruined.

From man's side, holiness had been displaced by sin, obedience by rebellion and self-will. Toward his God, fellowship had been displaced by enmity, love by fear, peace by guilt. Where once man was free, now he was held enslaved. Where once there was life, now death reigned.

From God's side, acceptance toward His man had been replaced by rejection, friendship by hostility, favor by wrath, approval by judgment. Where once there was blessing, now the curse of death.

No longer did man have access to God. Cherubs and a flaming sword guarded the way back into the Garden while it still remained on the earth. And from then on in Scripture God is seen with angelic guards about Him, keeping all that is unholy from Him. When the prophet Isaiah beheld God in His glory, seraphic guards were keeping His way about the throne, crying "Holy, Holy,

---

1. Eph. 2:3; 4:18; 2:1; Col. 1:21; Rom. 3:11b; Jer. 9:6b; Gen. 3:8; Job 21:14-15; Rom. 1:30; Col. 1:21

19

Holy".[1] In both the tabernacle of Moses and the temple of Solomon, cherubim of beaten gold guarded the throne from intruders, positioned with wings spread over the "mercy seat" where the Presence of God dwelt. Also upon the veil itself, which severely restricted what little glimpse of God by man that was allowed and that "not without blood", were cherubs embroidered—again as silent guards about the Presence of the Holy One—thus signifying that the way into the Holy Presence "was not yet made manifest".[2] All these proclaimed one thing: God is holy and unholy man is **BARRED** from His Presence!

But hallelujah! Into this desperately pitiful situation the Son of God was sent. Leaving the throne of God for a season, He was born as a man into this wretched earth, humbling Himself, and becoming obedient unto death, even the death of the cross. His purpose was to rend the cherub-adorned veil, from the top to the bottom, and to make a way of restoration possible for His beloved man to Himself.

In order for this to happen, God had to accomplish two things: the **legal penalty** of man's sins had to be paid, and man's **inward nature** had to be changed. Through the shedding of His own precious blood, Jesus paid an infinite price that far exceeded the entire penalty of all the sins of all men. Then through the new birth, administered by the cherished Holy Spirit, man's spiritual nature can be changed, and life birthed where there was only death, and man restored to an inward capacity of fellowship with God, the cry of "Abba, Father" being born within our hearts. Furthermore, through the baptism in the Holy Spirit, God Himself comes to dwell not just "with" His redeemed children but actually "in" them, our blood-washed bodies

---

1. Is. 6
2. Heb. 9:7-8

becoming "the temple of the living God", His "habitation (or, dwelling place) ... through the Spirit", our calling to "be filled with all the fulness of God".[1]

> *Having therefore, brethren, boldness to enter into the holiest by the blood of Jesus ...*
> *Let us draw near with a true heart in full assurance of faith (Heb. 10:19, 22)*

Praise be to the Most High Lord Jesus! Through the glorious work of the cross He has made a way back to God for man. By the shed blood of Jesus, man has a way of entrance through the former veil into the Presence of God. What was impossible, Jesus has made possible. The way to fellowship, communion, yea friendship, yea intimacy with God has been opened again to man; and we are invited to partake, and commissioned to invite others to partake of the highest and greatest privilege possible: the **marriage** of the Lamb and His bride.

The Highest Privilege

Listen to the bride of Christ: "the King hath brought me into His chambers".[2] The King of Kings has brought us in—into His Most Holy Place, into His innermost chambers of fellowship, into the deepest experience of His intimate communion. This is what He is offering us.

Jesus is calling us to **know** Him, as a wife knows her husband; and He is calling us to **enjoy** Him, as a wife enjoys her husband. Hear again His bride: "I am my Beloved's, and His desire is toward me ... His left hand

---

1. 2 Cor. 6:16; 1 Cor. 6:19; see also Eph. 2:22 and 3:17-19
2. Song of Sol. 1:4

should be under my head, and His right hand should embrace me ... I sat down under His shadow with great delight, and His fruit was sweet to my taste."[1]

And even more wonderful are the words of her Master, the Bridegroom: "Thou art beautiful, O my love ... Thou art all fair, my love; there is no spot in thee ... Thou hast ravished my heart, my sister, my spouse; thou hast ravished my heart with one of thine eyes ... Turn away thine eyes from me, for they have overcome me ... How fair and how pleasant art thou, O love, for delights!"[2] As in human marriage, so the communion and enjoyment in the relationship between Jesus and His bride is **mutual**.[3]

Then consider these words of the bride: "I am my beloved's, and **my beloved is mine**."[4] Did you read that? We are not only invited to know God and to love Him and to behold His lovely face for ever. We are called to **possess** God! In all that He has given us, in the great eternal promises He has made us, do not overlook this one supreme promise, this one ultimate gift, this one consummate inheritance—God has given us **Himself**.

A treasure greater than the sum total of the universe, of realms both seen and unseen: **God has given us Himself!**

And with what measure has God given Himself to us? Let us hear and marvel at the words of John: "God giveth not the Spirit by measure".[5] God has given Himself to us

---

1. Song of Sol. 7:10; 8:3; 2:3
2. Song of Sol. 6:4; 4:7, 9; 6:5; 7:6
3. As the Apostle John wrote, "we have fellowship one with another". (1 John 1:7)
4. Song of Sol. 6:3
5. John 3:34

22

without measure! All of God is in us—in each one of us! All of God is accessible to us—to each one of us! **All of God is ours!**

Then let us wonder at the words of Paul whose prayer is that "Christ may dwell in your hearts ... that ye ... may be able to apprehend with all saints what is the breadth, and length, and depth, and height; and to know the love of Christ, which passeth knowledge, that **ye might be filled with all the fulness of God**"![1]

Dear brother or sister, do not be satisfied with just looking and marvelling. Seek to **apprehend** this! Seek to **experience** this! **All of God is ours! All of God is yours!**

Promise of promises! Joy of joys! Wonder of wonders! Purpose of purposes! Indescribable grace! Matchless condescension! To know Him; to love Him; to possess Him! Eternity will not fathom the depths of the glory and wonder of the purposes of God, nor exhaust His praise.

This, then, is God's purpose and our calling: the fullest and most intimate union between ourselves and His Son—to enjoy Him forever.

To enjoy Him!

Forever!

---

1. Eph. 3:17-19

Draw me to Thee, till far within Thy rest,
In stillness of Thy peace, Thy voice I hear—
For ever quieted upon Thy breast,
So loved, so near.

By mystery of Thy touch my spirit thrilled,
O Magnet all Divine;
The hunger of my soul for ever stilled,
For Thou art mine.

For me, O Lord, the world is all to small,
For I have seen Thy face,
Where Thine eternal love irradiates all
Within Thy secret place.

And therefore from all others, from all else,
Draw Thou my soul to Thee ...
Yea—Thou hast broken the enchanter's spells,
And I am free.

Now in the haven of untroubled rest
I land at last,
The hunger, and the thirst, and weary quest
For ever past.

There, Lord, to lose, in bliss of Thine embrace
The recreant will;
There, in the radiance of Thy blessed Face,
Be hushed and still;

There, speechless at Thy pierced Feet
See none and nought beside,
And know but this—that Thou art sweet,
That I am satisfied.

(Gerhard Tersteegen)

CHAPTER THREE

The Difference Between Knowledge and Experience—the Reality of Fellowship

For the law having a shadow of good things to come, and not the very image of those things, can never ... make the comers thereunto perfect. (Hebrews 10:1)

The fellowship that was God's original intention in creating and then redeeming man, is a real fellowship—an actual experience of fellowship. Just as Adam walked and talked with God in the Garden in the cool of the day, so those who have been graciously restored to a state of peace with God should not be content merely to discuss the Christian life and to theorize about it, but they should be satisfied with nothing less than actually experiencing what Jesus died to make possible: a genuine communion and fellowship with the eternal God.

It is true of all of us that our knowledge exceeds our experience. To some extent in each of our lives, the things we know about God—His power, His holiness, His love, His being—go far beyond what we have personally experienced of Him. Many ears have heard of God, but few eyes have seen Him.

This breach between head-knowledge and heart-experience is a dissatisfying thing—or at least God **wants** it to be.

By offering glimpses of Himself to our mind's comprehension, God intends to inspire in us a seeking after the experience of the same things that we understand—a longing that we not merely be acquainted with Him, but that we experience intimate fellowship with Him. One of the reasons why God approaches our minds to give us a mental understanding in the first place is to direct our energy of seeking. This seeking, when it is finished, will attain His desired goal for us which is the true **experiential** knowledge of Himself.

God wants the discrepancy between our intellectual knowledge of Him and our heart experience of Him to **frustrate** us, in the sense of provoking us to dissatisfaction with a purely theoretical and academic Christianity, and prodding and goading us to seek an experiential and **real** Christianity.

At times, however, we have all made the mistake of receiving the knowledge, the mental comprehension, without also yielding to the Divine impulse to **seek**. This omission is not so bad in itself as it leaves open the future possibility of coming to a place of seeking. What **is** bad is when we have, for whatever reason, avoided altogether the seeking while substituting the intellectual theory for the life-experience.

Then when we present the theory of a particular spiritual truth to others and do not ourselves yet possess the experience of that truth, we will only impart what we possess; namely the theory alone. If the theory has become an adequate substitute for the experience in our own lives, then that will be all we impart to others—a **substitute.**[1]

And this substitute is harmful and quite spiritually debilitating when we are **satisfied** with it, because we deceive ourselves that we have the genuine experience

---

1. George Whitefield declared: "I am persuaded the generality of preachers talk of an unknown and unfelt Christ. The reason why congregations have been so dead is because they had dead men preaching to them."

when all we really do have is an intellectual comprehension of the theory about the experience. But since we mistakenly believe we already possess the experience, we find in our hearts no inspiration nor even **need** to seek for the reality of the experience. Thus enamored with our own religious ideas, we become lovers of philosophical doctrines more than lovers of God, all under the guise of "truth".

Our knowledge, which should have been good in propelling us to seek the experience, turns on us and slays us, robbing us of the experience—**robbing us of God!**

The Word of God Will Bring Us to Its Author

Jesus died to bring us to God, to restore us to fellowship with God. His death was not a theological construct but a fact; and so is the relationship with Himself and His Father that He purposed should be ours through His death.

We dare not reduce the Christian life to a mere theory of legal standing. We think we are "staying with the Word", but we are **NOT** staying with the Word, because **the Word of God points us to God, to the reality of Christian experience of God.** We who make our boast of the Word, let us not through disregarding the Word dishonor God.[1]

No, we are not saying that our legal standing with God is not relevant nor important. He **has** given us a glorious judicial standing of righteousness before Himself; but that is not the whole story. It was necessary for God to give us a legal standing before Him, just so that He **could** give us an **actual** standing before Him.[2] That is His desire: not that we content ourselves with discussing and

---

1. cf. Rom. 2:23
2. Gal. 4:4-6

debating our purely judicial right-standing with God, but that we earnestly seek the only thing that will really satisfy a born again heart, which is the true fellowship of love with God that He intended from all eternity.

We must free ourselves from the constraints of our Western culture at this point. Inheriting the attitude from the Greek philosophers Socrates and Aristotle, our culture puts a premium on **education**. The educated man is honored as the good man; the unschooled and ignorant man is pitied as the fool. Only an educated man can be happy and fulfilled. Knowledge is the supreme goal of our Western society. Information has become an end in itself. Reason is supreme. Man's intellect is sufficient. Scholarship is equated with maturity.

This perspective has unfortunately been carried over from the world into the church,[1] so that it has become more important for us to understand doctrines about God, than it is to experience Him and to be changed by Him. Knowledge in itself has become sufficient to us. Experience of God is seen as something only those few weak ones with a "mystical" bent ever pursue. This whole attitude has spelled tragedy in the church, and the great predominance of religious knowledge without living relationship with Jesus is a fundamental cause of the frequency of pride, carnal sectarianism, debate, strife and spiritual "blood-letting" in the true Christian community today.[2]

The world has never known God through its human scholarship and wisdom, and neither will we by those means.[3] We will never work, nor think, our way up to God. The Gospel of the Apostles was not with excellency

---

1. The infection of Christianity with Greek philosophical values began in the third and fourth centuries.
2. see 1 Cor. 8:1-3; 1 Tim. 1:3-7; 6:3-4; 2 Tim. 2:14; Tit. 3:9
3. 1 Cor. 1:21; 3:18-20

of speech nor with wisdom of words, but it was in demonstration of the Spirit and of power. It was with the movings and the conviction of the Holy Spirit upon the hearts of men.[1] The wisdom they did speak was **spiritual** wisdom coming by revelation from God.[2]

This wisdom is not the boastful wisdom of the labor of the human intellect, but it is the wisdom that the Holy Spirit, by **revelation**, teaches to a surrendered heart; communicating spiritual things by spiritual means.[3] Hidden from scholars and revealed only to "babes", this wisdom is **foolishness** to even the wisest of the world.[4] The natural man is not **able** to understand this wisdom which can only be "spiritually discerned";[5] and neither are Christians who walk and think and approach spiritual matters as natural men.

The Word of God is given to man as a means to bring us to Jesus; to bring us to know Jesus; to bring us to experience Jesus; to bring us to a life of obedience to Jesus; to bring us to a fellowship of love with Jesus. Our knowledge of the Word of God should not be an end in itself. It should be a **means** to a greater end: the personal experience of Jesus. The experience of the love of God "passeth knowledge".[6] We must not be satisfied with a merely academic understanding **about** redemption and **about** God; we must seek to **experience** redemption and to **know** God and to **be known** and **changed** by Him.

This will not be accomplished through restless academic exercise, but it is **only** as we **behold** the "glory of God in the face (and Presence) of Jesus Christ", that we

---

1. Rom. 1:16; 1 Cor. 2:1-5; 1:17; 4:20; 2 Cor. 1:12; 1 Thess. 1:5
2. 1 Cor. 2:6-12; see also Col. 1:9; Ps. 119:18; 147:19-20
3. 1 Cor. 2:13; Eph. 1:17-18; Matt. 16:17; Ps. 25:14
4. see Matt. 11:25-27; 13:10-11; Ps. 25:14; 1 Cor. 1:23
5. 1 Cor. 2:14; Rom. 8:7
6. Eph. 3:19

will be changed into His image by the Spirit of the Lord.[1] Without this experience, our Christianity will be more a change of opinion than a change of heart and life. Without this experience, we will only ever possess the outward "form" of knowledge and of Truth[2]—**real** knowledge, **real** Truth is in the inward parts. Truth will bring **life**. Truth will change our hearts. It is the very "Breath" of God.

The Balance of the Christian Life

Our knowledge of the Word of Truth has many God-ordained purposes, some of which are as follows. Firstly, our knowledge of the Word of God, by the revelation of the Holy Spirit, should lead us into the personal experience and knowledge of God. "And we know that the Son of God is come, and **hath given us an understanding, that we may know Him** that is true".[3] Then, our knowledge of the Word will help us to understand and articulate that experience.[4] Finally, our knowledge will guard our experience by protecting us from false influences.[5] But our knowledge was never intended to **supplant** our experience.

We must possess **both** the knowledge of the Word of God, **and** personal fellowship with the God of the Word. Those who have knowledge without experience will be fruitless and dry, their lives satisfying to neither themselves nor God. But those who seek only experience without the Word, often end up in a state of vague disorientation, being led more by impulsive flights of fancy than by Divine inspiration. Let us have **both** knowledge and experience.

---

1. Gen. 32:24-31; 2 Cor. 4:6; 3:18
2. Rom. 2:20; 2 Tim. 3:5
3. 1 John 5:20
4. 2 Tim. 3:16; Ps. 111:10
5. see Acts 17:11; Ps. 19:11a; Gal. 1:8; Ps. 119:11

Then our knowledge will lead us into true fellowship with God. In turn, our experience of God will lead us into a deeper understanding of His Word.

Here is the balance of the Christian life. The Word of God leads us to God, who in turn will reveal His Word to us, which points us again to Him and deepens our fellowship with Him. Thus we experience genuine spiritual growth and maturity. This is true knowledge and true experience. True knowledge of the Word will **always** lead us into personal experience of God; and true experience will **always** point us to, and be in accord with, the Word of God.

So we see that knowledge is to work in harmony with our personal experience of God. But our knowledge was never intended by God to be a **substitute** for our experience. We must not let it become this in our lives.

Come to His Word With a Surrendered Heart

If we approach the Word of God striving after knowledge either for the purpose of self-promotion in the eyes of men, or to learn how to live the "Christian life" apart from a living union with Him, then its study will not profit us. But if we approach His Word as babes, with surrendered hearts, sincerely seeking to know Him, then God will reveal His Word which in turn will reveal Him and bring us into personal fellowship with Him. It will be this **fellowship with** God—and not our **knowledge about** God—that will be the source of all joy and fruitfulness in our lives.

But if you, like many in this hour, have allowed your knowledge to become a substitute for heart-experience in your life—if you have used the Word to give you knowledge to live the "Christian life" apart from a lively fellowship with Him—then please have the honesty and the

31

spiritual courage to admit your need and your true lack. Stop the religious charade. It is often hard for men and women who have spent their lives in their own "religious education" and who may even have prominently taught others, to admit that the bulk of their endeavors has produced little but wood, hay and stubble. Nevertheless, if you refuse to acknowledge your need, you will hinder God from coming to you and bringing you to a place of genuine fellowship with Himself.

Christianity **is** the restoration of man to realized fellowship—to intimate union—with his God. If we are not pursuing this **supremely** and experiencing this **genuinely** in our lives, then we are not pursuing Jesus but some other religion of man. Furthermore, it is not true knowledge we possess, but some other kind.

We realize that by some this attitude will no doubt be seen as denigrating the Scriptures. This, however, is not to denigrate the Scriptures, but to **exalt** them. What greater praise could be made of the Word of God, than to declare that, by the revelation of Holy Spirit, it contains the power to lead a man to the simplicity of a true fellowship of love with the infinite God and Creator of all things?

Oh, Holy Scriptures! Oh, glorious Word! Oh, precious gift of God to men! Thou that would lead us into the very Presence of the Infinite One, who alone is able to keep us from falling and to present us faultless before the Presence of His glory with exceeding joy. Oh, faithful Word; if only we will, in child-like simplicity, believe and obey thee! How well Jesus' words to the religious experts of His time are fulfilled in this our shallow day of sophisticated theological dryness:

> *You search the Scriptures; for in them ye think ye have eternal life: and **they are they which testify of me.***

And ye will not to come to me, that ye might have life. *(John 5: 39-40, Greek)*[1]

When these same religious leaders confronted Peter and John after the day of Pentecost, they perceived that by their standards the two Apostles were "unlearned and ignorant men". Yet marvelling at their boldness and the spiritual authority with which they spoke, they recognized the true source of their spiritual wisdom and power: Peter and John "had been **with Jesus**".[2]

The early Apostles received their **motivation** to preach, their **qualification** to preach, and the **content** of their preaching, not from formal, didactic religious training but from their years of **personal fellowship with Christ**. Certainly Jesus did spend a lot of time teaching His disciples, but at the heart of their "Christian life" (and also at the heart of His teaching to them) was their daily walk with Him, their constant communion and fellowship with Him, their years of sacred intercourse with Him—their personal experience of **Him**.

They beheld Him; they touched Him; they talked with Him; they lived with Him; they loved Him; and they experienced His love for them. That fellowship was the simple **source** and **nature** of their "Christianity", and of all their future ministry to others.

Furthermore, as we will see, they went preaching the Gospel not just for the purpose of giving their hearers a collection of information about the principles of Christianity, but also to bring them into the real fellowship with God they themselves enjoyed. When they presented the Gospel they sought to make known to the people not just the Doctrine of Christ, but also "the **power** and **Presence**

---

1. cf. Acts 13:27
2. Acts 4:13; cf. Mark 3:14; John 15:27

of our Lord Jesus Christ".[1] That was their stated purpose in preaching the Good News!

God's ultimate aim for His people is that they know Him, and love Him, and experience Him and enjoy Him.

Jesus' longing is that His people see Him,[2] **hear** His voice,[3] **smell** Him,[4] **taste** Him[5] and **touch** Him.[6] Obviously the experience we are speaking of here is not an outward physical one but an inward spiritual one. Yet, to our spiritual senses, it is just as **tangible** and just as **real**. Our calling is not just to a legal relationship with our God, but to an **experienced fellowship**.

Do not settle for less than what God has intended for you from all eternity. Anything less is a bowl of pottage, a morsel of meat. Anything less is Christian existence and not Christian life.

Let us give up our Christian existence, and embark upon an experience of Christian **life!**

---

1. 2 Pet. 1:16 (the Greek word translated "coming" in this verse, literally means "Presence"); cf. Matt. 22:29
2. 2 Cor. 3:18
3. John 5:25; 10:3, 27
4. 2 Cor. 2:14-16
5. 1 Pet. 2:3
6. 1 John 1:1-3.

CHAPTER FOUR

The All-Inclusiveness of Fellowship

*That which was from the beginning, which we
have heard, which we have seen with our eyes, which
we have looked upon, and our hands have handled, of
the Word of Life;*

*(For the Life was manifested, and we have seen
Him, and bear witness, and shew unto you that
Eternal Life, which was with the Father, and was
manifested unto us;)*

*That which we have seen and heard declare we
unto you, that ye also may have fellowship with us:
and truly our fellowship is with the Father, and with
His Son Jesus Christ. (1 John 1:1-3)*

In the beginning of the first chapter of his first epistle, the
Apostle John sets forth his principal motivation in preaching the Gospel. And it was not his motivation only, but it
has been that of all true servants of God, then and since.

What could this motivation be to cause these men to
endure hardships, persecutions, beatings, stonings, impris-
onments, journeys, perils, shipwrecks, misunderstandings,
betrayals, weariness, painfulness, watchings, hunger and
thirst, fastings, cold and nakedness? What could this
passion be that those consumed by it would forsake all
worldly fortune, pleasure and pursuit in seeking to take the
Gospel to others? Surely it must be their concern for man's
deliverance from an eternal hell? Surely no other purpose
could justify such sufferings as the true servants of God
have experienced historically? But, no, this was not their
primary motivation.

Stated here in First John is the reason why these men proclaimed the Gospel to us; namely, that we may have fellowship "with them", meaning that we may have the **same** fellowship that they had, and that "is with the Father, and with His Son Jesus Christ".[1] Here was their passion, their all-consuming obsession, and the deepest desire of God's true servants in this our day: **to bring men to the personal knowledge of Jesus Christ and the Father.**

Furthermore, please notice what the fellowship is that John wants us to experience. Is it a purely theoretical knowledge of God that we should have? Is it simply an academic appreciation of the Biblical doctrines about the Son of God that we need strive after; merely an accurate understanding of the legal, judicial implications of the teachings of the New Testament that we must endeavor to achieve? God forbid!

John says that we should pursue the same **fellowship** with God that he experienced. And what quality of fellowship was that? Listen closely as the Apostle himself tells us about his own relationship with God, which level of relationship he desires that we all experience: "That which was from the beginning (i.e. the eternal God), which we have **HEARD**, which we have **LOOKED UPON**, and our **HANDS HAVE HANDLED**, of the Word of life". Here was the reality of John's experience of God: he heard Him, he looked upon Him and he even **touched** Him! This was

---

1. John said not that his fellowship "was" with God, but that his fellowship "is" with God. Through the indwelling Holy Spirit, John experienced a vital union and communion with Christ long after Jesus had physically left the earth, and his objective was that we know that **same** fellowship.

John's fellowship with his Lord. It was real. It was tangible. It was an intimate fellowship with his Master.[1]

John touched the eternal God, his hands handled Him! He rested his head upon God's bosom. Obviously John had no physical contact with eternal, infinite, transcendent Spirit, yet he **DID** touch God. Great is the glory and the mystery of godliness: God was manifested in the flesh, and dwelt among men. The eternal God whom no man can look upon and live; the great infinite Spirit who dwells in light unapproachable; the unchanging, omnipotent, omniscient, omnipresent Creator of the universe was born of a woman and tabernacled among us. This is the glory and the wonder of the Incarnation. The invisible God now has an Image. The Father whom no man has ever seen is now revealed.[2] Emmanuel walks among men.[3] Man once again has personal fellowship with his God.

This is why John preached the Gospel: that we might be restored to fellowship with God; and not just to a legal, theoretical relationship with God, but to a fellowship as solid and as "tangible" as the intimate friendship that John himself enjoyed with the Saviour.

In fact we have been called to an **even deeper inward fellowship** with God than what Jesus' disciples enjoyed while He was on the earth:

---

1. Part of John's reason for these words was to combat the error of Cerinthus, who taught heresy concerning the Person of Christ. His theory was essentially a denial of the full and true union of both God and man in Jesus Christ. He taught that the "Christ-spirit" did not actually inhabit the human Jesus until the baptism, and then left Him before His death on the cross. To remove this error in the minds of the people, throughout his epistle John stresses the reality of both the Deity and the Humanity of Christ. Jesus was and is **fully** man and **fully** God. To know the man Jesus, is to know God.

2. Col. 1:15; Heb. 1:3; John 14:7-9; 15:24

3. Hebrew for "God is (personally present) with us"

*It is **expedient** for you that I go away: for if I go not away, the Comforter will not come unto you; but if I depart, I will send Him unto you ... I will not leave you comfortless: I will come to you. (John 16:7; 14:18)*

We may be tempted to be jealous of the companionship the disciples had with our Lord, but really we are not offered anything less than what they had. The communion we can experience with Jesus through His indwelling Spirit, is more abiding and far more intimate than a mere physical closeness. This is what we are called to. Our summons from the Great Eternal King is to know Him, to experience Him, to enjoy Him, to possess Him.

*God is faithful, by whom ye **were called unto the fellowship of His Son** Jesus Christ our Lord. (1 Cor. 1:9)*

This is what the Christian life is: restoration to fellowship with God. The experience of this should be our highest aspiration.

The Christian Life is in Jesus

Unfortunately, the church today is filled with goals that fall far below this great purpose. But if we will set our face toward the single pursuit of the personal knowledge of Jesus, we will discover that it is an all-embracing pursuit.

Our pre-eminent call is unto God. **He** is the highest and the all-encompassing call to the Christian. **He** is our

38

salvation. **He** is our life.[1] To know Him is our goal, our ultimate purpose. And when we have Him, we have **all He is**. When we have Him, we have **everything**. Eternal salvation, healing, deliverance, eternal security, peace, joy, holiness, righteousness, faith, the fruits of the Spirit, spiritual strength and power—all are in Him. Do not seek for anything outside of Him. In **Him** we are complete, and can do all things—and without Him we are empty, and can do nothing.[2]

Let us come to know Him first and the rest will follow. And without coming to know Him first our lives will not bear the genuine fruit of the Spirit, but instead we will produce only counterfeit **religious-looking** works of the flesh. Furthermore our lives will be satisfying to neither ourselves nor God.

To illustrate, let us consider for a moment some of the objectives that are held high in Christian circles.

Take holiness and obedience, for example. We shall now examine the fact that true holiness and righteousness, and the service of obedience to God can only be produced **subsequent to** a personal restoration to God and experience of fellowship with Him.

Everyone knows that a Christian is to be holy and righteous. For many, holiness is the pre-eminent purpose of the Christian life. But what is holiness? Does holiness consist solely in external works? What about the unsaved ones in the community who live outwardly clean, upright, moral lives—are they "holy"? Is a life pleasing to God simply because outwardly it conforms to a long list of religious "do's and don'ts"?

Anyone who has read the Sermon on the Mount knows that there is more to holiness than mere outward works,

---

1. Ps. 35:3; Col. 3:4
2. Col. 2:10; Phil. 4:13; John 15:4-5

and that true holiness must begin with the attitudes and motivations of the heart. Furthermore, Jesus' words in Matthew chapter twenty-three to the scribes and Pharisees, offer the sternest rebukes to those who, ignoring the true state of their heart, think themselves to be holy and righteous on the basis of outward works alone. Obviously, therefore, in our search for true holiness and righteousness, the first place we should look must not be outward works, but the heart.

So the question becomes not so much one of outward actions, but rather: **has the heart been changed** from that of fallen Adam? Has the spirit of man participated in the life of God? Is holiness now the **desire** and the **love** of the **heart**? The only testimony that pleases God is: "I delight to do thy will, O my God: yea, thy law is within my heart."[1] This is true holiness and righteousness: that which springs spontaneously from a changed heart. There is not the duty of holiness for this heart, but the joy. Righteousness is not a constraint but a pleasure. Serving God is not a hardship but a privilege. This heart's attitude toward the will of God is not "I must", but "I want to", and it is found only in those who have been truly restored to God, whose religion is not for the purpose of pleasing men but pleasing and enjoying God.

The key to true holiness is to experience and to know God. The key to Divinely-pleasing righteousness and obedience is union with Divine life. When our hearts possess the life and movings of the Spirit we will overcome the flesh. Our only source of spiritual victory is the true inward knowledge of Jesus. Our only source of genuine power is the abiding influence and Presence of God. As William Law wrote, "nothing godly can be alive in us but what has all its life from the Spirit of God living and

---

1. Ps. 40:8; 73:1; 111:2; 112:1; 119:47

breathing in us." Or, to put it in the words of Jesus: "As the branch cannot bear fruit of itself, except it abide in the vine; no more can ye, except ye abide in Me."[1]

Whatsoever is **born** of God overcometh the world. It is the reality of the inward working of God in a Christian's heart that will give him the direction, motivation and strength necessary for his Christian life. Jesus said the Kingdom of God is as seed hidden in the ground. The organic life within the seed is the power that causes the growth of the tree. Or again, the Kingdom of God is as a small portion of leaven hidden in a lump, which though small eventually saturates the whole. The potency of the inward life of the Holy Spirit within the born again heart is what permeates and transforms the Christian's whole life.[2]

Christianity is the restoration of man to fellowship and union with His God. Out of this inward union, the Christian life grows. Out of this partaking of the life of Christ Himself, is generated that same life within the believer:

> *Except ye eat the flesh of the Son of Man, and drink His blood, ye have no life in you ...*
>
> *He that eateth my flesh, and drinketh my blood, dwelleth in me, and I in him.*
>
> *As the living Father hath sent me, and I live by the Father: so he that eateth me, even he shall live by me. (John 6:53, 56-57)*

In our own strength and ability we **cannot** reproduce His life and image in our lives—**but He can!** Man, in himself, is not **able** to live a life that is holy, righteous and faithful, and therefore pleasing to God; but the Christian

---

1. John 15:4; cf. Ps. 92:13-14
2. 1 John 5:4; Matt. 13:31-33

life comes easily and naturally to the life of Christ. "There is none good but One, that is, God."[1] When **His** life abides within, godly outward actions will follow.

> *This I say then, Walk in the Spirit, **and** ye shall not fulfill the lust of the flesh.*
> *For the law of **the Spirit of life** in Christ Jesus hath made me free from the law of sin and death.*
> *And **if Christ be in you**, the body is dead because of sin; but the Spirit is life because of righteousness.*
> *... if ye **through the Spirit** do mortify the deeds of the body, ye shall live.*
> *For as many as are **led by the Spirit of God**, they are the sons of God. (Gal. 5:16; Rom. 8:2, 10, 13b-14)*

Holy works are simply the outward expressions of the Presence and life within us of the Holy One. What else would a true relationship with He who **is** holy produce but a genuine holy life? This is not out of religious duress nor coercion, but just as the growing of fruit or flowers on the branches of a tree is the spontaneous and natural outgrowth of the life within the root of the tree, so all true outward works of holiness will spring spontaneously and naturally from the seed of inward fellowship with holy Divine life.

> *Whosoever abideth in Him sinneth not: whosoever sinneth hath not seen Him, neither known Him. (1 John 3:6)*

If there is sin in our lives it is not because "we are not trying hard enough" . The Apostle John says it is because we have not **seen** and **known** God; it is because we are not

---

1. Mk. 10:18

abiding in Him. That is our solution—union and communion with Him. **He** is our solution.

True holiness and righteousness are the fruit of union and communion with God, and they cannot be produced apart from that. We repeat, true holiness and righteousness cannot be produced apart from a changed heart, which in turn cannot be produced apart from encounter and fellowship with God. The efforts of those who try to force holiness from a heart that has never truly met Jesus are destined to failure.[1]

True holiness and righteousness are "organic". They are not a mask that can be put on and off, but a skin that grows from the life and substance within and cannot easily be removed.

We will never be able to achieve holiness in our lives without first entering into a personal fellowship of love with the Holy One. To even attempt it is as futile as trying to put a piece of new cloth on an old garment or new wine into old wineskins.

Furthermore, the exercise is as **unpleasing** to God as it would be to a husband for his wife to have the task of dutifully serving him without first ever falling in love with him, and without first ever coming to intimately know him. Her service is forced and driven, and she resents every minute of it. But she has committed herself to marriage and knows it is for life, and so she must go round and round upon the treadmill of her wifely duties; all along complaining and murmuring, consumed with the bitterness of her plight. It would be even worse if she secretly desired her own career—her labor for her husband being not at all her desire but merely something she has been taught she **must** do.

---

1. see Matt. 15:18 & John 3:6

Service without submission and love is **bondage,** and it is not gratifying to the slave nor to the master. That is **not** the Christian life! God accepts no slaves but slaves of love. He neither needs nor wants the obedience of men whose only motive is guilty religious compulsion. He desires **first** our love and our fellowship, and then true obedience and holiness in our lives will naturally follow.

Our service to God must not be performed "grudgingly, or of necessity". Only the "willing heart" is a "perfect heart" before the Lord.[1] And it is only the heart that has beheld Jesus in His glory and in the "beauty of His holiness", that will be willing to obey Him, and that will **desire** His life and His holiness and His virtues. And only when we desire His perfections will we empty ourselves for His perfect life to come and dwell within us, so "the beauty of the Lord our God (may) be upon **us**".[2]

So we see that encounter with God is the womb of desire for Him, which in turn must precede all service for Him. The service that results from this will not be that originating from a self-serving need for dead religious works, but it will be born of a lively fellowship with God in His perfections.

It is only as we "with unveiled face **behold** ... the glory of the Lord (that we) are transformed into the same image from glory to glory ... by the Spirit of the Lord."[3] **He** is our path to holiness. **Fellowship with Him** is the fountain-head of all our Christian qualities. **Beholding Him** is the source of all our Christian character.

So it is with every one of the "expected" fruits of the Christian life. Faith, for example, is not really faith at all unless it is the mere spontaneous consequence of a personal

---

1. 2 Cor. 9:7; 1 Chron. 29:9; cf. Ps. 78:7-8
2. Ps. 90:16-17; 149:4b; John 17:22
3. 2 Cor. 3:18; cf. 1 John 3:2, 6

relationship with the Faithful One; again not out of guilt nor constraint nor perceived religious duty, but the mere natural result of a sincere fellowship of love with God.

We will only really trust one whom we know. Those who **know** God will put their trust in Him.[1] We will only be able to truly put our trust in the Lord, if we have first drawn near to Him.[2] If our religion is mostly theoretical and we lack **personal experience** of Jesus, then we will never be able to trust Him, no matter how many times we exhort each other that faith in God is our obligation and responsibility. The true Christian life is not that we must **try** to trust Him: it is that through His gracious self-revelation and His indwelling life we **may** trust Him, and we **are enabled** to trust Him.

Jesus' yoke is easy and His burden light.[3] Like feathers to a bird, holiness should not be a burden to us but a blessing. Like wings to a butterfly, faith should not be our load but our help.

To put it another way, let us paraphrase and amplify the words of the Apostle Paul in the first few verses of Romans chapter eight: Those who have received the gift of eternal life, towards whom God has no judicial condemnation, are not under the law. And yet the righteous requirements of the law will still be fulfilled in them and reflected in their lives. Because they are in Christ—simply because they are genuinely in Christ and He in them—they **will not** walk after the flesh but they **will** walk in the Spirit.[4]

This truth is also presented in the Gospels. When Jesus forgave the sins of those who came to Him, He also transformed their natures and **delivered** them from sin:

---

1. Ps. 9:10
2. Ps. 73:28
3. Matt. 11:28-30
4. see Rom. 8:1-4

... Neither do I condemn thee: go, and sin no more. (John 8:11)

This is Christian **life**, and it is Christian **liberty**. True liberty in Christ consists in liberty from bondage to sin and death.[1] The basis of Christian liberty is a heart that has been changed and restored and made alive to fellowship with God. This heart will not use its liberty for an opportunity to ignore all knowledge of holiness and truth and indulge the flesh;[2] but, now dead to sin and **alive to God** in the Spirit, it will long for further depths of fellowship and communion with God. This heart will not ask what is allowable, but rather what is honorable and good—not what can be gotten away with, but rather what will nourish one's fellowship with God. As a matter of course this heart will avoid anything that would displease God or grieve Him away; and the **natural compelling desire** of this heart will be obedience and faith towards God, and love towards the brethren.[3]

Come to God!

My brother or sister, if you know you lack the fruits of the Spirit in your life, then the answer does not lie in "trying to grow them". The remedy does not lie in greater discipline, increased resolution, more self-control nor just plain trying harder. The answer lies in **coming to God**. The fruits of the Spirit will spontaneously issue from a

---

1. Gal. 5:1; John 8:34-36; Rom. 6:7
2. Ps. 119:45; Gal. 5:13; Tit. 1:16; 2:11-12; 1 Pet. 2:16; 2 Pet. 2:19; 1 John 1:6; 2:3-6, 29
3. Gal. 6:15; 5:6, 13-14; see also Eph. 1:15; Col. 1:4; 2 Thess. 1:3; 1 Tim. 1:5; Philo. 5; 1 John 3:23

heart that has been changed and restored to fellowship with God.[1] **COME TO GOD!** Give Him your heart! That is what your need really is.

We do new Christians the gravest of injustices when we teach them how to "play the part" of a Christian without giving them the inward reality of experience of Jesus Christ. We teach them how to act "holy", how to live "righteously", and how to talk "faith", and then require it all of them. But unless we have in truth actually **led them to Jesus Christ** who will be the only true **inward Source** of all these fruits, we have only succeeded in teaching them how to **imitate** the Christian life, and have not at all helped them to become real Christians. We have taught them how to display the outward forms of godliness all the while neglecting the inward power thereof. We have done little more than to bring them into religious captivity.

This produces several classes of Christians. On the one hand are those who play along with the game, mouthing all the right things and learning how to climb the religious ladder of church acceptance and respectability— "professional Christians". They become expert at making the right moves, and all their spiritual exercise is stereo- typed and based on approved convention rather than simply being the outgushing of a genuine fellowship with God. They profess spirituality, but possess very little. Others will **see** and **hear** their Christian lives but no-one will **feel** them.[2] Their hearts are empty, and their lives barren, while outwardly they smile and play the part. Unfortu- nately, these self-motivated souls are often the ones who end up as leaders in the world of organized religion.

On the other hand, those who are not satisfied with imitation, and who are honest enough to admit to

---

1. see Gal. 5:16-25
2. As one brother said, "You can't get warm by a painted fire!"

themselves that in their own strength they are unable to live the life anyway, eventually become discouraged and disheartened. Some of these will consign themselves to accept a miserable life of mediocrity and substandard Christian experience. They know in their heart there is more, but do not know quite what it is nor how to rise above defeat to obtain it.

A lesser number, who cannot stomach such a life of lukewarmness, and over whom the temptations of the world have a greater pull, will tragically fall away to their eternal destruction.

A final group is really only a part of this last group. However for them dissatisfaction with the burdens of "playing Christian" and "playing church" leads them not to accept defeat nor to fall away, but out of disillusionment there dawns a need to press on to know God and to find what their heart tells them is lacking. According to the degree of their frustration will be the intensity of their agony, and the depth and sincerity of their search for God.

If the Christian life primarily consists in the restoration of man to inward fellowship with God and union with His life, then should not our principal concern for new converts be that they come into this experience? Furthermore, we will then find that every aspect of the Christian life that we want to see them come into will be taken care of naturally and in due course. **Our greatest passion for young Christians must be to bring them to Jesus!**

Please understand, we are not implying that we should not teach new Christians or encourage them towards holiness and faith. The teaching of the Scriptures, and godly exhortation, are of **great** importance to their growth.[1] But what we are emphasizing is that due to the inadequacies of our own walk with Jesus what we impart to babes in the faith, too often, is little more than a "head knowledge" of doctrine and historical facts, and a set of beliefs and ethics that they know they should agree with and adhere to.[2]

However, if we expect them to truly grow and bear fruit, we must give them **Jesus**. This will not only be accomplished through teaching and exhortation, but our lives themselves must become the epistles of Christ, written by the Spirit of the living God; so proclaiming and revealing the crucified Christ that others will see Him and be drawn to Him. It will not be a mere telling of others about Jesus—He will be **revealed** in His people.[3]

This is the function of the true church of God. Jesus' church is not a religious meeting once or twice a week in a certain building that a group of individuals attend, but it is a living united fellowship that one is birthed into by the Holy Spirit. It is the twenty-four hours a day, seven days a week, life and fellowship of the saints one with another— in Him—in His life and fellowship. This is the true church and in it is the true revelation of the Lord of the church. This is how Jesus will be manifested to men: living and abiding in His church. And when they see Him they will be drawn to Him—not to a denomination, nor to a creed nor

---

1. Matt. 4:4; John 6:63; Acts 20:28; Rom. 15:14; 2 Cor. 7:1; Col. 1:28; 1 Thess. 4:1; 1 Tim. 4:13, 16; 2 Tim. 2:2, 19; 3:14-17; 4:1-4; Tit. 1:9

2. Unfortunately, teaching—which, in itself, is right and good—if it is not accompanied by an experiential leading of the people to Jesus, can become a **distraction** from what is pre-eminently important: namely that the saints come to know personal fellowship with Him.

3. 2 Cor. 2:14-15

doctrine, nor to a set of morals and ethics, but to **Him**. We must give them **Jesus**.

If we will **love** Jesus Christ with all our heart, soul, mind and strength; if we will trust Jesus for **everything**; if we will eat, drink, work, play, worship, pray, sing, teach, sleep, breathe **Jesus**; and if we will get down in the dust beside new converts and pray them through into a real personal **encounter** with Jesus;[1] then they will be changed by Him, and they will come to know Him, and they will come to love Him, and they will come to trust Him, and they will come to obey Him, and their lives will bear fruit remaining unto eternity.

If we can bring them to Jesus Christ, **then** they will come to a true knowledge of holiness. If we can bring them to Jesus, **then** they will believe Him whom they come to know to be faithful. If we can help them to experience a relationship of love with God who is Love, **then** they will come to have a true burden for a lost and dying world, as well as a deep capacity of love and forbearance toward the saints. This is our calling to the world: we are to help men to **BE** reconciled to God, not just to teach them how to act like it.

The true fruits of the Spirit are not just mechanical "learned" responses that a Christian knows he should provide at certain times, but they are the unfeigned spontaneous outgrowths of union and communion with God. They are not "taught" conditions of the mind, but rather Divinely-imparted graces of the heart.

We must stop teaching unholy people how to act holy, and instead take them by the hand and lead them by way of the altars of abandonment and surrender into the Holiest of All—into the very Presence of the Almighty around whose throne seraphs eternally cry "Holy, Holy, Holy". This

----

1. Gal. 4:19; Col. 1:29-3:3; 4:12-13

personal confrontation with He who **IS** holy will implant a holy seed within them, which of itself will bud and grow into holy works and a fruitful life that is pleasing to God.

Simply to mouth holiness and to act holiness when our hearts are filled with rebellion and self-will is not at all pleasing to God. He wants Truth in the inward parts—and the inward parts will only be changed by encounter with God and the impartation of His life.

Faith is Nurtured by Fellowship

It is the same with faith. As we have said, you will only trust someone you know. You will only greatly trust someone you know intimately. If you have never met a certain man or woman, you will not trust them a great deal. You may trust them with little things, or concerning things that are not all that important to you, but you probably will not trust them with anything major.[1] Furthermore, the source of your confidence in them will not be a third party telling you how trustworthy they really are— although that may help—but it will be primarily your own personal experience of them as you come to know them and they are confirmed to your heart as indeed being faithful and worthy of your trust. "Such faith", as Charles Price wrote, "is not the child of effort, neither is it born of struggle." But such faith is the mere natural and inevitable consequence of personal fellowship.

So it is not "more faith" in God that you need—you need more of **Him**. And when you have more of Him you will have more faith—it will simply be there.

---

1. Or at least, you should not!

So then, faith cometh by hearing, and hearing by the Word of God. (Rom. 10:17)

The "hearing" Paul speaks of here is not the hearing of the proud religious intellect,[1] but the hearing of a surrendered heart turned completely towards God. It is only through the reception of the Word of God in a yielded heart that we come to know Jesus, and to the extent that we know Him we will trust Him. To put it simply: faith comes by knowing God, which in turn comes by hearing and receiving His Word which is His revelation of Himself.

And His Word will only be truly received by a heart which is abandoned to Him. Those who have never genuinely forsaken all to obtain Jesus have not yet begun to know Him, no matter how religious they may seem to be. So to teach them how to act like they have faith in God and how to talk like they have faith in God, when they have not sincerely given their lives into His faithful hands, and when they have not yet begun to develop a significant personal experience of He who would be the object of their faith, is to invite disaster.

Jesus is the Author and Perfecter of our faith.[2] Our personal experiential knowledge of Him and our faith in Him are inseparable. Faith that is purely academic, consisting in nothing more than mental assent with Scriptural principles that may in themselves be sound, is not authentic faith and in times of trial and testing it will **always** fail. A true faith will triumph and abide forever,[3] and it is only present in the hearts of those who know Him, to whom faith is not a requirement or duty but a privilege.

---

1. cf. verse 21; see also Heb. 3:7-19
2. Heb. 12:2
3. 1 Cor. 13:13

It's All in Him!

*Abide in me, and I in you. As the branch cannot
bear fruit of itself, except it abide in the vine; no more
can ye, except ye abide in me.*

*I am the vine, ye are the branches: He that abid-
eth in me, and I in him, the same bringeth forth much
fruit: for without me ye can do nothing. (John 15:4-5)*

Before we can expect to see the growth of Christian
character and fruit in our lives, we must first encounter
God. We must first come to know Jesus inwardly and
personally. Anything else is false, external religion and a
worthless substitute for Christian reality. Anything else will
never satisfy: either us or God. Anything else is of no
value.

It is only through our personal union and communion
with Jesus that Christian fruit will be produced. As we
increase in the knowledge of Him, so will the fruit of our
lives increase.[1] Only the fruit that is birthed in our fellowship with God will remain.[2] Only the works that are built
upon the foundation of our personal knowledge of Jesus
Christ will endure. Everything else is wood, hay and
stubble.[3] Of everything else God asks, "Who hath required
this at your hand?"

Some lovers of man's religion, whose main task in life
seems to be to coerce new converts, through the means of
guilt and fear,[4] into conforming to externals, may argue
that this appears to offer a license to sin and live in

---

1. Philo.6; 2 Pet. 1:3
2. John 15:4-5
3. 1 Cor. 3:11-13
4. It is not our purpose here to deal with the true Fear of the Lord.
It will be the subject of another book.

unbelief toward God.[1] To them we reply that the real sin of unbelief is to perpetuate the spawning of "imitation" Christians who have never given themselves to Jesus, who have known very little encounter with God, who have never really "tasted" of the Lord, and whose Christianity consists solely in religious duties and an outward identification with a church and a set of beliefs, ethics and doctrines.

The Lord has not sent us to discourage new Christians and to deceive the world with this falsehood, but to proclaim the Gospel of Truth. And the Gospel is the power of God unto restoration with Himself—nothing more (what could be more?) and nothing less.

God has told us that the Christian life can only be found in Christ Himself. "Without me ye can do nothing." Why do we not believe Him? When will we cease from our own vain religious labors, and instead direct all our energies toward **Him**? True Christian character will only be produced out of a living, vital, inward union with its Source: Jesus Christ Himself.

Jesus is the Source of Everything

Everything is in Jesus. Do not seek anything outside of Jesus. He died on the cross to restore you to Himself. He did not die to deliver you from Hell; He died to restore you to Himself and in Him you will not see Hell. He did not die that you may be healed; He died to restore you to Himself, and in Him you will find a most marvelously capable, compassionate and infallible Healer. He did not die to give you a life of prosperity and protection; He died

---

1. see Gal. 4:29-30; 5:11-12 and 6:12-13

to restore you to fellowship with Himself, and in Him you will be gloriously protected and provided for.[1]

Jesus did not die that you may live a righteous, ethical life; He died to restore you to Himself, and in union with Him your heart will be captivated by the beauty and invigorated by the power of Divinely-imparted holiness. He did not die that you might be bound with a life of religious busyness and duty; He died to bring you to Himself that you may know the delightful privilege of living every moment in His gracious fellowship and sweet service.

So let **Him** be your desire; purely to behold and to know Him your longing. Be captivated with **Him**; and not just so you will receive anything from Him or can do anything for Him. But seek communion with Him simply because He is precious. Worship Him merely because He is God and you are man. Let Him become your song just because He is worthy. Long for Him for His own sake. Hunger for Him for no motive other than **Him**. Thirst for Him because only **He** can ever satisfy.

And when you come to this place—when you will seek Him and Him alone for no other motive than to behold Him, to know Him, to love Him and to worship Him—then you will find all the rest abundantly provided for. This is God's order. This is true religion.

We need **nothing** beside Jesus. "Without Him was not anything made that was made." He is the **Source** of all things, the **Sustainer** of all things, His glory the **purpose** of all things. What need do we have that He cannot fulfill? What other solution to **anything** is there but Him? What other reason for anything is there but Him? What foolishness that we should seek anyone or anything other than Him!

---

1. see Ps. 91; 17:8; 18:2; 31:20; 32:7

As Elder Brooks once wrote to John G. Lake, "I did wish to just hold up Jesus and make you look at Him from every angle and see how transportingly beautiful He is—how all sufficient He is—how He fills all—meets every requirement—satisfies every longing—is Himself the equipment for every service. Oh, John Lake, there is no other need of ours in this world or that to come but Jesus ... Oh, my Brother John, I once looked for **power**—wanted **equipment**, sought **usefulness**—saw gifts in the distance—knew that dominion was somewhere in the future, but glory to God! One by one these faded, and as they faded there was a **form**, a figure emerged from the shadows which became clearer and more distinct as these other things faded and when they had all passed I saw 'Jesus only'."

Jesus is our Glorious One, our Holy One, our Perfectly Beautiful One, our Majestic One who is clothed with strength, honor and splendor, our Beloved, our Chiefest among Ten Thousand, our Most Excellent One, our Altogether Lovely One, the One who Himself is our Glory, whose greatness is unsearchable, whose Name alone is exalted, whose glory is above the heavens and the earth, the First, the Last, the only One worthy of all our heart and thoughts.

He is the Fountain-head of all glory and beauty; the Storehouse of all fragrance and purity. Set your gaze upon Him. You are His, and He is yours. Let your cry be after the closest intimacy and union with Him: "Let Him kiss me with the kisses of His mouth". Let **Him** be your obsession, your captivation, your preoccupation. Be immersed in Him. Be engrossed in Him. Be absorbed in Him. For no other reason than Himself.

King David said it this way:

One thing have I desired of the LORD, that will I seek after; that I may dwell in the house of the

LORD all the days of my life, to behold the beauty of the LORD, and to inquire in His temple. (Ps. 27:4)

David's desire was to look upon His Lord, to contemplate His beauty, to dwell in the house of the Lord. "As for me, I will behold thy face".[1] To David the place of God's manifest Presence was the "perfection of beauty", the "joy of the whole earth". He delighted in His Lord. He took pleasure in His Lord. He adored the Pre-incarnate Son of God. He wanted simply to be with Him, to look upon Him, to know Him, to love Him, to worship Him, to enjoy Him. That was David's end, the highest purpose of his life. This is the heart fully turned towards the Lord, of which God Himself testifies that it is "perfect" before Him.[2]

You were created by Him and for Him. **He** is your end, your **ONLY** purpose. He created your heart to desire, love, enjoy and worship **Him**. Only **He** can ever satisfy your deepest need. No matter what it is that you lack in your life, your real lack, your real need is **Jesus**. In truth, He is your **only** need. It is all in **Him**. Pursue **Him**. The rest will follow. And, dear friend, even if it does not follow, what will you care? Your heart will be complete and content in **Him**.

The cause of our difficulties is that we seek His gifts, His works and His ways, while ignoring **Him**. But what is the sense in looking for light or heat and disregarding the sun! What is the rationality in searching for water and neglecting the ocean?

Forbear seeking His and instead seek Him! Cease seeking anything but Him. He is the beginning and the end. There was nothing before Him, and there will be nothing after Him. No matter what your need, you must seek His

---

1. Ps. 17:15; 2 Sam. 7:18; Ps. 65:4
2. 1 Kings 15:3; 1 Sam. 13:14; Acts 13:22

face. Your answer is nowhere else obtainable. He is your Infinite, Unlimited, Eternal Source of everything. In Him you are complete.

We Have No Need Other Than Him

So where we have sought "holiness", "faith", "the fruits of the Spirit" and all the other hallmarks of the Christian life let us instead now pursue **Christ**. Let us find Him and simply walk with Him. Then one day we will look at our lives and to our eternal joy we will see real holiness, real faith and the true fruits of the Spirit. No longer will all those things elude us, but we will have them—simply because they are all in Him and **we have Him**.

Are you seeking deliverance from demonic oppression, seemingly unable to find it? Seek Jesus and in Him you will discover a mighty Deliverer who shall set you free indeed. "Mine enemies ... shall fall and perish **at thy Presence**." God's instruction is to submit ourselves to Him **first**, and **then** to resist the devil in **His** power and strength and authority.[1]

Are you seeking healing for your body? Dear friend, it is far more important, and incomparably more profitable, to seek to make contact with the Healer than it is to seek the healing. In **Him** is healing. All who look upon **Him** shall live. "As many as **touched** (Him) were made perfectly whole." Look not to "faith formulas" nor to "the power of your mind" nor to other methods or means of receiving healing apart from a living connection with Him. Look only to Him. Jesus is your Healer. Jesus is your

---

1. Ps. 9:3; 68:2; Jam. 4:7; Ps. 56:9

Healing. Touch Him and He will make you whole. Receive Him and His life will be your health. **He** is your need.

Are you seeking Divine guidance for your life? Jesus taught that those sheep who know the Good Shepherd will perceive His voice.[1] Strive to know Him, seek **Him** first of all, and His will shall be clearly revealed to you in due course. He Himself shall be a light unto your path.

Are you trying to endure faithful to God until the end? Come to know Jesus, and in His fellowship and by His power you will be kept until that Day when you will be presented faultless and blameless before His glory with exceeding joy. He Himself will be your "strong habitation, whereunto (you) may continually resort". He upholdeth those who follow hard after **Him**.[2]

Are you seeking joy? Seek it no longer. Jesus has been anointed "with the oil of exultant joy" above all others. Seek Jesus and in Him you will be filled with joy unspeakable and full of glory. "In thy Presence is fulness of joy; at thy right hand there are pleasures for evermore."[3]

Are you seeking peace in this world of tribulation and turmoil? Set your affection, your attention, your trust, and your heart fully upon Jesus, and an abiding "perfect peace" shall be yours.[4]

Are you seeking knowledge and understanding? Jesus **is** the Truth. You will never come to any knowledge of Truth apart from knowing Him. In Him "are hid all the treasures of wisdom and knowledge".[5] Only through the apprehension of Jesus will these treasures ever be revealed.

---

1. John 10:4, 14, 27; 8:12; Acts 13:2
2. 2 Tim. 1:12, 14; Jude 24; Ps. 71:3; 63:8; John 17:11
3. Heb. 1:9 (Greek); Ps. 16:11; 21:6
4. Is. 26:3; John 16:33
5. John 14:6; Col. 2:3

Do you desire spiritual light and freedom from error? Then look to Him. **His life** is "the light of men", and it will **not** be overcome by darkness.[1]

"The Truth is in Jesus". True understanding is found only in His Presence.[2] Jesus **is** the Truth. You do not "have" Truth simply because your head contains some ideas about Christian doctrine or "Judæo-Christian values". You will only know the Truth when you have abandoned all to come to know **Him**.[3] You only possess Truth when your heart pulsates with the life and Presence of Jesus. Seek Him and you will know the Truth, and the Truth will set you free.

True spiritual maturity is not a maturity of religious scholarship but a maturity of intimacy with God.[4]

Yes, you should have sound doctrine, but not apart from having **Him**—not divorced from knowing **Him**—not separate from union and communion with **Him**. "God ... hath in these last days spoken unto us **by His Son**".[5] Jesus is the Revelation. He **Himself** is the Truth. He is the Word, the Logos, the Revelation and Expression of God. Do not seek to possess any system of "truth" without possessing Him. He—**His Person**—is the Truth. You **cannot** know Truth apart from a vital experience of Him—a living union with Him.

Are you seeking the blessings that are yours through the work of the cross? Seek instead "the living God, who giveth us richly all things to enjoy". "They that seek **the Lord** shall not want any good thing." "Delight thyself also in **the Lord**; and He shall give thee the desires of thine heart." "Seek ye first the Kingdom of God, and His

---

1. Jn. 1:4-5
2. Eph. 4:21; Ps. 73:17
3. see John 7:17
4. see 1 John 2:13a
5. Heb. 1:1-2

righteousness; and all these things shall be added unto you."[1]

Do not seek the blessings apart from Him! Should you obtain them, without Him they would mean nothing but anguish and vexation of spirit; while with Him even your greatest sufferings and deprivations will be sweet.

Are you seeking the gifts of the Spirit? Do obey His Word and desire the best gifts, but **not** as ends in themselves, and **not** before you possess Him. Seek Jesus and in the richness of His fellowship He has promised you an abundance of gifts as they are necessary. It is "by Him" that you will be enriched "in everything ... in all utterance, and in all knowledge ... so that ye come behind in no gift".[2]

Are you seeking to enter into a life of intercession on behalf of others in the church and in the world? Seek Jesus, and in communion with our great High Priest you will experience the blessed privilege of participating in the depths of **His** intercession. In union with Christ, His burden will become your burden, His travail your travail, His groanings your own. Thus it will not be in your own strength but rather by His mighty inward workings that you will labor and agonize, waging effective warfare according to the power of His Spirit.[3] This union with Christ in His travail and intercession is one of the highest privileges of fellowship with Him that you are offered in His Presence.

Are you seeking unity in the body of Christ? Hear the words of Jesus: "**I in them** ... **that** they may be made perfect in one". And again, as He prayed to His Father, "that they also may be one **in us**".[4] The only source of

---

1. 1 Tim. 6:17; Ps. 34:10; 37:4; Matt. 6:33; see also 2 Pet. 1:2-3
2. 1 Cor. 1:5-7; cf. John 3:2
3. Rom. 8:26; Col. 1:28-2:3; 4:12-13; Gal. 4:19
4. John 17:21-23

true unity within a church is the indwelling life of Christ within His people.[1] Without the reality of that life, **all** attempts at achieving unity on whatever basis—love, evangelism, doctrine,[2] lack of doctrine, pure will-power, etc.—will be utter failures.

Indeed without the reality of the indwelling life of Christ, the very existence of the church itself has no point nor spiritual value. The church that the Holy Spirit birthed is a living breathing organism expressing the life of Jesus which throbs and courses within its spiritual veins. And as the body without the spirit is dead, so this land is filled with "churches" that, pitifully destitute of the life of Christ, are little more than barren religious organizations; reflecting little more than the talents, abilities and dispositions of their leaders; glorifying little more than the ambitions and aspirations of their founders; and fulfilling little more than some eternally-fruitless social function in their community.

This tragic state of affairs can be transformed by only one thing: the restoration of individual Christians to God, and the recovering of the life of Jesus within the heart of the believer. Are you seeking church life? It is only in Jesus that it can ever be found.[3]

Are you seeking ministry in these last days? Strive to know God and you **will** be used in a wonderful end-time harvest and move of God upon this earth, but make **Him** your first and only desire. "The people that do know their God shall be strong, and do exploits."[4]

Do you understand what we are trying to say? God is "a Rewarder of them that diligently seek **Him**". Do not

---

1. see Eph. 4:3-6, 13
2. Rom. 14:1-15:7
3. Ps. 127:1
4. Dan. 11:32

seek anything of the Christian life outside of Him. Do not try to live the Christian life outside of Him. "As you have therefore received Christ Jesus the Lord, so walk ye **in Him**". The Christian life is not found outside of Jesus. It does not exist apart from Him. If you do not have Him, you have nothing of any value. And when you have Him, you have it all.

Our only end—our only purpose—is the Lord Jesus Christ; and in Him we are **complete**.[1]

Let **Him** be your pursuit.

---

1. Col. 2:10

As pants the hart for cooling streams,
When heated in the chase;
So longs my soul, O God, for Thee,
And Thy refreshing grace.

For Thee, my God, the living God,
My thirsty soul doth pine;
Oh, when shall I behold Thy face,
Thou Majesty divine?

(Nahum Tate & Nicholas Brady)

CHAPTER FIVE

The Pursuit of Fellowship

O God, thou art my God; early will I seek thee:
my soul thirsteth for thee, my flesh longeth for thee in
a dry and thirsty land, where no water is;
　　To see thy power and thy glory, so as I have seen
thee in the sanctuary. (Ps. 63:1-2)

The fellowship of God is the most precious thing in the universe. **Do not think God gives it lightly!** By this we do not mean He requires us to work in some way and earn His fellowship, because it is certainly given by grace, and we could never do anything to deserve it anyway. In ourselves we will never merit anything before God. All that He gives us is on the grounds of Jesus' blood alone and is imparted as a totally free gift. But while God grants His fellowship freely, yet the fact is, He only gives His fellowship—His deep intimate fellowship—to those who **desire** it, who desire **Him**.

Each of these complementary truths is expressed in the same verse by the prophet Isaiah:

*Ho, **every one that thirsteth**, come ye to the*
waters, and he that hath no money; come ye, buy, and
*eat; yea, come, buy wine and milk **without money and***
***without price**. (Is. 55:1)[1]*

---

1. see also Jn. 7:37-39; Matt. 5:6; Ps. 107:9; Rev. 22:17

In the realm of human relationships, while you give your fellowship freely, yet you only fellowship with those who desire your fellowship, don't you? Or do you force the deepest expressions of your innermost thoughts and feelings on those who have absolutely no desire to know anything about you? In the same way, God reveals Himself only to those few, that "little flock", who truly desire Him.[1] And the depth to which He will reveal Himself to you will be determined by the depth of your passion to pursue Him.

Desire is the appetite of the soul. The greater our desire to know Him, the more we will turn from everything that would steal our attention from Him, the greater will be the space we make in our hearts for Him to come and fill, and the greater will be His response of fellowship. This does not mean He loves us any more, but simply that we experience and enjoy Him more.

God wants to reveal Himself to all His children in a deep and profound way. None will be left out if they are willing to yield to Him. Few, however, desire Him enough to sufficiently empty themselves for Him to come and fill.

Those who will know God, will first have desired Him. They will first have hungered for Him. They will first have thirsted after Him. Their souls will first have broken for the longing they have for Him.

> *As the hart panteth after the water brooks, so panteth my soul after thee, O God.*
> *My soul thirsteth for God, for the living God: when shall I come and appear before God? (Ps. 42:1-2)*

---

1. cf. Matt. 13:10-16

This Cry is Within You

If you have been born of God, if you have His seed—His life—within you, then this cry is already deep within your heart. And it is calling to the deep within His heart. "Deep calleth unto deep". Do not try to find this cry somewhere. Just resist it no longer. It is there. Simply allow it full expression. Give it full throat. Yield to it. **Quench not the Spirit**. Cry after God. He will draw near to those who cry after Him. He will fill those who hunger for Him. He will give Himself to those who desire Him.

> *My soul **longeth**, yea, even **fainteth** for the courts of the LORD: my heart and my flesh **crieth out** for the living God. (Ps. 84:2)*

This cry is within you. It is not only a cry **to** God: it is a cry **for** God. "My heart and my flesh crieth out for the living God." Your heart longs and cries for God; and, if you will yield to your heart then your flesh will cry for God—that is, you will actually physically do it.[1]

"My flesh longeth for thee in a dry and thirsty land, where no water is". This is the greatness of the cry of those who desire God. This is the extremity of their longing. In a land where **no** water is, what would be the response of your body? Very soon, after less than a single day, it will begin to **demand** water. Then, if this demand is not quickly met, your body will begin to **seek** for water. If this search is not soon concluded it will begin to **call** for water. If this call is not quickly answered, it will begin to **shout** for water; and if this shout is not quickly responded to, your body will begin to **scream** for water.

---

1. cf. Matt. 12:34b

67

What **acuteness of agony** will be yours, what **desperation!** This cry will not come merely because you feel you **should** cry for water, but it will arise naturally and spontaneously, unsolicited from the depths of your being. You do not have to **try** to thirst for water if you have been in a hot land of drought and have not drunk anything for several days! Your thirst and your cry are not things you have learned to do. You were **born** with these responses. They are innate. They are natural. They are uncontrived and unfeigned.

God made you to thirst, because your body's first, most basic and most important need is for water. Without water you will die. If your body is denied water it will begin a response of self-preservation: it will begin to **cry.** Because of the requirements of dignity and decorum you may be able to contain this cry for a while, but if your thirst is left unquenched, eventually you will **scream.** Eventually nothing else will matter—not your dignity, nor your self-respect, nor others' opinions of you. Neither will you be concerned about the "pose" you strike as you go about it. Your single all-consuming obsession will be your **need** for water. You **must** have water. You **must** have water or you will **die.**

Even so, religious propriety is abandoned when the soul realizes—truly realizes—its deep need of God. When confronted with its true state of lack and spiritual drought, the heart's cry for God becomes more than a polite and mannerly response to religious instruction: it becomes **real.**

I stretch forth my hands unto thee: my soul thirsteth after thee, as a thirsty land... (Ps. 143:6)

This cry is a cry for God; it is a cry for life. It is not just a cry for knowledge. In a desert would knowledge about the chemical nature of water be of any use to you whatsoever? Even so, the cry within you is a cry for God

Himself. For God to come to you. For God to reveal Himself to you. For God to draw you into His Presence. For God to satisfy the longing of your heart with the only thing that **can** satisfy the heart of man—**Himself**. Man's religion will not satisfy. Scholarly pursuits will not satisfy. Self-deception will not satisfy. The praise and acclaim of men will not satisfy. You **must** have God.

You were born with this cry within your heart.[1] You **must** have God. You **must** have God, or else your life in this world will be one of living death: "thou hast a name that thou livest, (yet thou) art dead".

God has made you with the faculty of spiritual thirst, because your pre-eminent need is for Him. He made you to thirst, for without Him you will die. You must have Him. "My soul thirsteth for **thee**". He alone can satisfy. He alone can fulfill your deepest need, because your deepest and most basic need, whether or not you fully understand it, is for **Him**—to know Him, to love Him, to obey Him, to fellowship with Him, to enjoy Him, to worship Him.

Cry After God!

This is the cry that you know is deep within you. The enemy of your soul has used religious pride and your own self-sufficiency to stifle it, but allow him to do this no longer. If the thirst is ignored, the desire will remain yet unsatisfied. If the cry is permitted to be smothered, the need will remain yet unmet. If the root is not allowed water, the plant will not only fail to bring forth fruit—it will die!

---

1. By "born" we mean "born again", of course.

To the inevitable charge of "emotionalism" we reply that a man dying of thirst in a desert is not so much concerned with decency and acceptability in the eyes of others as he is with finding water for his life. His scream for water is his scream for his life.

So cry after God! You **must** have God! Set Him before your face. Cry that He would rend the heavens and come down. Seek the Lord fervently. Pour out your heart like water before Him! Lift up your soul unto Him. Cry to see Him. Cry to know Him. Cry to have Him. Cry to possess Him in all His fullness. Cry after God! Cry after God! **Cry after God!** "Your heart shall live that seek God."[1]

---

1. Ps. 69:32b

CHAPTER SIX

The Nature of Fellowship—the Depths of the Love of God

Then ... a lawyer asked Him a question ...
saying, Master, which is the great commandment in
the law?

Jesus said unto him, Thou shalt love the Lord thy
God with all thy heart, and with all thy soul, and with
all thy mind.

This is the first and great commandment.

And the second is like unto it, Thou shalt love thy
neighbour as thyself.

On these two commandments hang all the law and
the prophets.

... there is one God; and there is none other but
He: And to love Him with all the heart and with all
the understanding, and with all the soul, and with all
the strength, and to love his neighbour as himself, is
more than all whole burnt offerings and sacrifices.

... love is the fulfilling of the law. (Matt. 22:35-
40; Mark 12:32b-33; Rom. 13:10b)

God is Love: infinite Love. To dwell in God is to dwell in Love. To fellowship with God is to fellowship with Love. To know God is to know Love: true Love.

To experience the love of God for us is the greatest encounter any man can have, and to return love to Him is the greatest privilege any man will ever be allowed. To partake of both this encounter and this privilege is what it means to be a Christian.

71

The Christian life is a participation in the life and thus the love of God. This is what we have been called to do: to receive God's love and to love Him. Furthermore, dear Christian, this is **ALL** we have been called to do. And when we love God, when we **truly** love God, it will follow that we shall please Him, even delight Him in every way. "Love is the fulfilling of the law."

The strength, yea the **substance**, of our Christian life is our love of God. This is the love that was birthed in us when we were born again. This is the love that will mature and grow throughout our lives, and that will usher us into the eternal Kingdom of God. This is the love that will keep us when nothing else will. This is the love that alone will fulfill all of God's requirements and expectations of us.

The source of our love for God is, of course, His love for us. "We love Him because He first loved us." "Draw me, we will run after thee".[1] Before we were born again, we did not at all love God—we hated Him. But He loved us, and Jesus died for us that we might be restored to Him. Upon the new birth and the baptism in the Holy Spirit, the love of God was poured out in our hearts.[2] We were restored to fellowship with God, and to a new life of love for Him. From this time on, everything in our life is to be motivated by a single rule: the power of our love for God.

Upon salvation, the love of God began in our lives, and according as this love flourishes and grows, so we grow and bear fruit in Christ.

In every action we have a choice of love: we must choose either the love of self or the love of God. We can only love and choose one; and when we love one we have by default hated and rejected the other. God can not and will not fellowship with self, which is at enmity with Him;

---

1. 1 John 4:19; Song of Sol. 1:4; John 15:5
2. Rom. 5:5; 1 Pet. 1:22-23

so our fellowship with Him will grow only as we renounce self and choose instead to love God.

As we love and obey Jesus, He will increasingly manifest Himself to us.[1] This growing fellowship is beautifully depicted in the book of Ezekiel.[2] The prophet saw a river that flowed from the Presence of God, and as God took him through the waters they became deeper and deeper until they were "waters to swim in".

So it is with our relationship with the Lord. As we walk with Jesus and lovingly trust and obey Him, choosing the love of God over the love of self, He will increasingly reveal Himself and His love to us. As we go deeper in our experience of His love for us, so our ability to return love to Him is enlarged. As we dwell in His Presence, the flame of love which He has planted in our hearts is fed and fanned. So it continues: in the fellowship of God we grow both in the capacity to love Him as well as to receive love from Him. The love of God swallows us up, becoming the dominating rule of our entire life.

Love is the Fulfilling of the Law

As we grow in our experience of fellowship with God, His love will increasingly rule us, and become the very substance and fabric of our lives.

The love of God will cause every action of obedience to God.[3] "And this **is** love, that we walk after His commandments." To confess to love God and yet to disobey Him is to make ourselves liars. Those who love

---

1. John 14:21
2. Ezek. 47
3. 1 John 5:3; 2:5; 2 John 6

73

God will abstain from even the appearance of disrespect and disobedience to the One they love.

Jesus said, "If you love me, you **will** keep my commandments."[1] Therefore obedience to God will inevitably spring from a heart that has set its love upon Him, and it will spring from desire, not duty.

The love of God will be the motivation for our separation from the world and its ways. "Know ye not that the friendship of the world is enmity with God? Whosoever therefore will be a friend of the world is the enemy of God."[2] The Kingdom of Heaven and the Kingdom of this world are of different **natures**, and the one **contradicts** the other. To love the one is, of necessity, to **forsake** the other. We cannot have treasure divided between the two Kingdoms.[3] What is highly esteemed by one is an abomination to the other; what is valuable to one is despised by the other; what is treasure to one is trash to the other. We only have one heart; we only have one affection; we can only serve one Master. And to love and serve that one Master **is** to hate and forsake the other. "For a day in thy courts is better than a thousand. I had rather be a doorkeeper in the house of my God, than to dwell in the tents of wickedness."[4]

To love God is to heartily and joyfully abandon all the ways of the world: fondness for position and respect; covetousness; pride and vanity of dress and fashion; pursuit of the pleasures, diversions and follies of this age; self-love and indulgence; trivial friendships; groundless strifes and divisions; idle talking; unprofitable occupations of time and money; and whatever else would characterize this world

---

1. John 14:15, Greek
2. 2 Tim. 4:10; 3:2-4; Jam. 4:4
3. Matt. 6:19-21
4. Ps. 84:10

74

and its lusts which are passing away forever. Your **love for God** will birth this course in your life. Do not try to forsake the world without first clinging to Jesus, or else all that will result will be dead religious legalism. **Love God** with all your being, and separation from this world and its ways will inevitably and naturally take place in your heart and then in your life.

The love of God will spurn entanglement with the things of this life. "If any man love the world, the love of the Father (i.e. his love to the Father) is not in Him." The cry of Jesus' bride will be: "Thy love is better than wine". All the pleasures and delights of a thousand lives are as a drop of the bucket, and are counted as the small dust of the balance when weighed against one moment of exchange of love and communion with the Highest. "Thy lovingkindness is better than life". "There is none upon earth that I desire beside thee." All the kingdoms of this earth are not worth relinquishing one moment of the heaven of worshipping and serving the Lord our God. Those who truly love Him will spend their lives on this earth as "pilgrims" and "strangers" seeking no permanent dwelling place here but looking only for the city whose Builder and Maker is God.[1]

The love of God will be the passion behind our unyielding faith in Him for all things.[2] To love God is to have our hearts so completely turned toward Him, our lives so entirely consumed in Him, that not to trust His abundant promises would be unthinkable. To love God is to abandon all we are and all we have into His care and His alone. To not trust God is to prove we do not know Him, for He **is**

---

1. 1 John 2:15-16; Song of Sol. 1:2b; Ps. 63:3; 73:25b; Matt. 4:8-10; Heb. 10:34; 11:9-10, 13-16, 24-26; 13:14; Gen. 47:9; 1 Chron. 29:15; Ps. 102:14; Matt. 10:37; 16:26
2. Matt. 6:19-33

trustworthy; and if we do not know Him, how can we say we love Him?

The love of God will be the wellspring for every act of love and mercy toward our brethren and toward all men. "If we love one another, God dwelleth in us, and His love (that is, our love to Him) is perfected in us."[1] The Apostle John taught constantly on love, so much so that, it was said, the people he taught grew weary of its incessant reiteration. His constant admonition was, "Little children, love one another." When asked, "Master, why do you always say this?", his reply was, "Because it is the Lord's commandment, and if only it be done, it is enough."

The love of God will motivate a life of faithfulness in all the "little" things of life. As Brother Lawrence wrote, "God does not regard the greatness of the work but the love (to Him) with which it is performed." When viewed from this true perspective our whole life becomes replete with activities in which we can render our love for Him. The distinction between religious and secular employments of time is lost, and all our endeavors—whether spiritual or menial—become opportunities for devotion to Him, and occasions for eternally-glorious expressions of obedience and fidelity.[2]

The love of God will spawn a life of generosity and self-sacrifice, both toward God and man.[3] In His great love for us Jesus gave all He had. What could be too great for us to give in our love for Him? "Beloved, if God so loved us, we ought also to love one another."[4]

The love of God will be our encouragement to joyfully endure the trials, sufferings and persecutions which are

---

1. Heb. 6:10; 1 John 4:11-12, 17-21; 5:1; 2:9-10; 2 Cor. 2:4
2. see Eph. 6:7; Col. 3:17, 23-24
3. 2 Cor. 8:7-24; 1 John 3:16-18
4. 1 John 4:9-11

such a necessary and vital part of our union with Christ.[1] If we long for Him we will submit ourselves to the fellowship of His cross, which is the only path to enter into the true knowledge of God we will ever have offered to us.

The love of God will be our provocation towards a life of holiness and righteousness.[2] To love God is to love all that He is. God is holy. If we truly love God and have beheld the beauty of His holiness, it will not be our burden but rather our yearning to participate in that most excellent of His perfections. And our yearning will be a fierce one. Without holiness "no man shall see the Lord". Only "the pure in heart ... shall see God".[3] Our love for God will not allow us to take lightly anything that could ever separate us from Him. As Smith Wigglesworth said, "Worldliness is that which cools my affection towards God". Those who love the Holy One will fervently do battle with the forces of the world, the flesh and the devil whose ruthless bent is to blur and ultimately destroy our fellowship with Jesus.

The love of God will precipitate our desire to preach the Gospel to the ends of the earth. The nature of the Christian life is the restoration of man to the experience of personal fellowship with his Creator, and this is the Gospel we should be presenting. If we have genuinely experienced this restoration ourselves it will be our earnest desire that others do also.

When we look at evangelism in this light its whole nature changes from what we have historically seen undertaken in the name of "world missions". Evangelism must spring spontaneously out of the reality of our fellowship with Jesus, and our love for Him. As a result we will

---

1. John 21:15-19; Rom. 8:28; Phil. 3:10
2. John 14:15, 21; Ps. 97:10a
3. Heb. 12:14; Matt. 5:8

never attempt to export our **religious culture** nor our **Western way of life** to other peoples and nations, but we will desire to take only **Him**. Furthermore, because we will not be promoting a certain doctrine, creed nor denomination, we will not be satisfied when those to whom we minister come to a place of mental agreement with our teachings or express a superficial confession of salvation, but we will seek first and foremost to bring them into the manifest reality of **a genuine experience of personal fellowship with Jesus Christ**.[1]

The love of God will also work in us a passion to see those converted presented to Christ in glory on the last day.[2]

An interesting story about the Apostle John is related by an Early Church writer. John once visited the city of Smyrna, and found there a sturdy and intense young man. "I deposit this lad in thy keeping," he said to the local elder, "with all earnestness, taking the church and Christ to witness." The elder accepted the trust and, when John returned to Ephesus, took the boy home, nurtured him, and baptized him. Then, thinking he had done enough, he let him alone, and the boy fell into evil company, committed a crime, and, fleeing to the mountains, became the captain of a band of robbers.

After a time John revisited that city, and after settling the business which had brought him, he said to the elder: "Now then, restore us the deposit which the Saviour and I entrusted unto thee". The elder was startled, supposing that he was being accused of some financial impropriety. "It is the soul of the lad that I am requiring," explained John, "and the soul of the brother." The elder groaned and wept:

---

1. This is how and why the Early Church turned the entire known world upside down in a few short years.
2. Eph. 4:15; Phil. 1:8-11; 3 John 4

"He is dead!" "How? When? And what death?" "He is dead to God," said the elder, and told the story. The Apostle rent his robe and with a loud cry smote his head. "A fine guardian of the brother's soul did I leave in thee! Let me have a horse immediately and some one to show me the way." And he rode off and found the lost youth, and by tender entreaties won him to repentance, and brought him back to the saints and to God.

The love of God will be our own energy to endure to the end.[1] No temptation, trial nor suffering could ever have the power to divert the enraptured heart from its ultimate goal of finally beholding the face of the One whom it so dearly loves.

The Kingdom is only promised to those who **love** Jesus.[2] Choose now, who and which kingdom you really desire. If you love Him you **will** endure—anything! "For love is strong as death; jealousy is as relentless and unyielding as Sheol: the coals thereof are coals of fire, which hath a most vehement flame. Many waters cannot quench love, neither can the floods drown it".[3]

The love of God will generate in our hearts a hunger to know, and a willingness to receive the Truth of God's Word.[4] The errors of man, and the lying doctrines of the devil will offer neither attraction nor satisfaction to the man or woman who loves Truth Himself.

The harvest of the Bible is Christ. That is why we love the precious Book—because it reveals Him whom we love and hunger to further know.[5]

This love will kindle in our hearts true worship of God in spirit and in truth, as well as sincere praise and

---

1. 2 Thess. 3:5; 2 Tim. 4:7-8; Heb. 3:14; 9:28; 1 John 3:3
2. Jam. 2:5; Ps. 69:36
3. Song of Sol. 8:6-7, Hebrew
4. John 6:42-47; 8:37-47; 3:19-21
5. Luke 10:38-42

thanksgiving to Him not only for His great salvation but pre-eminently for His great Person.[1] The Father "**seeketh such to worship Him**". This worship—true worship—is an end in itself. We were created to worship Him. He is God; we are His created beings—what other response could we have toward Him but one of unconditional surrender and worship? "O come, let us worship and bow down: let us kneel before the Lord our Maker. **For** He is our God; and we are the people of His pasture".[2]

Animals cannot worship God, because they were not made in His image. Only man can offer worship that is acceptable and pleasing in God's eyes. Unfortunately he rarely does. Despite the popular contemporary teaching, true worship is not just something we do to release the power of God for healings and deliverances and the meeting of needs in our services. While it is indeed true that the power of God will often be manifested spontaneously in the midst of the worship of His people, yet that should not be our reason for worship. We should worship God simply because we love Him, simply because we have beheld Him in our hearts: our precious, wonderful, worthy, Almighty God. Anything else is not true worship but self-serving attempts at flattery of Him.

Neither is true worship of God just for the purpose of preparing the hearts of the people for whatever will happen in the rest of the meeting; for example, the preaching of the Word. Again, worship certainly will have the effect of plowing up the ground of our hearts for the receiving of His Word, and yet it is still a question of ulterior motive.

Do we really think that the infinite God, who knows our hearts far better than we do ourselves, is pleased when we smile at Him and sweetly sing songs of love and

---

1. Luke 7:36-50; Ps. 70:4; 54:6
2. John 4:23-24; Ps. 95:6-7

adoration to Him while in reality we are but trying to **use** both Him and the exercise itself for our own purposes and ends?

Neither is true worship of God just singing memorized songs to fill up a traditional set period of time. But worship in spirit and in truth is **an end in itself**. True worshippers worship God "in spirit", and not in traditional outward forms and ritual—no, not even in traditional Charismatic or Pentecostal forms and rituals. And true worshippers worship God "in truth" and in reality, and not from an insincere, dishonest or manipulative heart. Worship is our pure, sincere, unfeigned and spontaneous response of surrender, love and adoration to our Maker, our Redeemer, our King, and our Lord. Anything from any other heart, or for any other motive, is nothing but "strange fire" before our God.

The love of God will beget a holy dissatisfaction with the religious systems of man, and a longing to see the restoration of the house of God—which is the true Church of the living God—the organic, innate, natural expression of the life of the Holy Spirit within His people—without ritual or ecclesiastical hierarchy—a living, breathing organism expressing the life and fellowship of Jesus Christ. "Lord, I have loved the habitation of thy house, and the place where thine honour dwelleth."[1]

The love of God will justify the forsaking of all things, even father, mother, wife, children, brethren, sisters and one's own life, just to gain Him. Our beloved has spoken, "and said unto (us), Rise up, my love, my fair one, and come away". So that we can cleave unto Him and be one with Him, we must first leave everyone and everything else behind. For God to be wholly ours we must give

1. Ps. 26:8; John 12:42-43; 1 Tim. 3:15; John 2:17; Matt. 21:12-13; Ps. 132:3-5

ourselves wholly to Him. "Yield to the Lord with simple heart, all that thou hast, and all that thou art". We must give all for All. But by those who truly love Him, **any** price to possess Him will be considered cheap.[1]

The love of God will be our end. The love of God will be our only endeavor, our only joy and delight—the full attention and satisfaction of our hearts. The love of God will be our life.

Any other reason or any other motive behind any thought or action in our lives will not be acceptable. The love of Jesus is our only law, our only requirement, our only obligation, our only responsibility, and our only **life** in God.

"Grace be with all them that love our Lord Jesus Christ in sincerity. Amen."

---

1. Luke 14:25-33; Song of Sol. 2:10; Phil. 3:7-8

CHAPTER SEVEN

The Community of Fellowship—the Church

And it came to pass, as He sat at meat with them,
He took bread, and blessed it, and brake, and gave to
them.
And their eyes were opened, and they knew
Him ... (Luke 24:30-31)

To understand the nature of the church we must first understand the nature of the Christian life on a personal level. In former chapters we have discussed the fact that the Christian life is the personal restoration of the individual believer to realized fellowship and communion with his God—it is nothing more nor less.

We have been restored to God. He saved us that we may experience union and communion with Him. To know Him—to experience intimate fellowship with Him—is our goal, our ultimate purpose. And when we have Him, we have **all He is**. We have everything. Salvation, healing, deliverance, eternal security, peace, joy, spiritual strength and power, holiness, faith, the fruits and gifts of the Spirit—all are in Him. And all will be imparted to us through union with Him.

Out of inward union and fellowship with Jesus issues **everything**: the whole of the Christian life. That is all the Christian life is—union and communion with Jesus. When we have Him we have it all, and without Him we have nothing of any value.

It is so with the church. Just as the Christian life is **union** and **fellowship**, even so the church is **union** and **fellowship**. Its nature is union. Its nature is fellowship.

83

Union and fellowship with Christ, and union and fellowship with each other—in Christ. That is all the church is: union and fellowship with each other, in Him. And every other aspect of church life will come out of that—inevitably and spontaneously. And it will be real. When it comes it will be genuine, and alive. Whatever comes of the church will not spring from organization, programs or any human effort or agency, but it will be the mere reflex action of the life of the Holy Spirit within His people.

Just as the individual Christian life grows inevitably and spontaneously out of personal fellowship with Christ, so church life, and all it consists in, springs inevitably and spontaneously out of personal fellowship with each other—in fellowship with Him.

One Loaf

The bread of communion is a beautiful type of this fellowship. In fact it so profoundly depicts the nature and life of the church that Jesus ordained it to be enacted and understood every time His people have a meal together.

Consider the loaf of bread. It, of course, represents Jesus. He is our life. His past death makes possible the way for our deliverance from destruction—both eternal and temporal; and His present indwelling life is the source of all our victory and life. He is our life. We live to the extent that we have partaken ("eaten") of Him. As we eat Him, so we absorb Him and He Himself becomes the very fabric and substance of our lives. He becomes not just our example and teacher, but in union with Him He actually lives His life in and through us. As we eat Him, we partake of His holiness, His love, His goodness, His faith, His power and all His attributes—His life.

Now notice: **the loaf of bread is eaten by all the saints—together!** In this there is wonderful significance.

Firstly, we see that **all the saints** partake of the fullness of the loaf. It is divided among them. No single believer eats **all** of Christ. We are each only given a **piece** of Him. Of course God is infinite Spirit and thus indivisible, and each "piece" of Him necessarily contains the whole of Him. But in His revelation of Himself to and through His body of believers—just like the loaf that Jesus broke and divided among His disciples—He gives Himself piece by piece.

Thus no-one can be independent of the others. It is only **together** that we have Him in His fullness. It is to the church as a whole that He gives Himself. Individually He reveals Himself to us in part and we partake of Him in part. We each stand in vital need of the pieces of the loaf that the other members of His church have digested into their souls and lives. Together we possess the **whole loaf**. It takes all of us together to reveal the fullness of the "absorbed" and indwelling life of Christ.

Thus the church **as a whole** grows up into the unity of the faith and "into perfect union with Him";[1] and **from Christ** "the whole body (is) fitly joined together and compacted by that which **every** joint supplieth, according to the effectual working in the measure of **every** part".[2]

Secondly, notice that the saints eat of Him **at the same time**. In the corporate life of the church comes the greatest experience of the life of Christ that will ever be revealed to us and that we will ever partake of.

It is in union with "**all** the saints" that we will apprehend the fullness of the Presence and the love of Christ. It is "ye" (plural—i.e. the church) who will "be filled with all the fulness of God."[3]

---

1. Eph. 4:15 Williams trans.
2. Eph. 4:16
3. Eph. 3:17-19

It is **together** that we experience Him. There are no "lone rangers" here. There are no individualistic ministries here. There are no individual spectators here. There are no individuals at all here. There is only the body—the one absorbed loaf—the one expression of the one indwelling **Life**—the one collection of believers who together inextricably form the whole—His church.

Our churches today are filled with individuals living their own separate lives. We are together, in a sense, once or twice a week under the same steepled roof. At least outwardly we are "together". Inwardly and spiritually we are islands; going our own separate ways; living our own separate lives. Our lives are not one—one with Him and one with each other, in Him.

The true church will be composed of individuals. But they are men and women who have heard the call to denial of self, and to union with Christ and His church. In Christ and in His church they have willingly and joyfully given up all right to the expression of their own self-centered lives and ministries. Interwoven with each other within the fabric of Christ's life they have become one. Each is indistinguishable from the whole. Their only life is as part of the whole. They only have meaning as part of the whole. Their own life is not their highest purpose. In seeking Him they have found His church. Christ's life expressed in His church is their highest purpose. They are "faceless" men and women.

But they are not without identity. Their identity is in Christ expressed in His church. Corporately their single face reflects His. Together they have partaken of His life. And His life has become theirs. Their life is one. It is His life. It is **Him**. He is their life—**together**. His life is their life—**together**.

This is what Jesus is restoring—the church—His church. All things He has ordained to this end. All things

He has planned from before eternity to work to this end—His church.

In Jesus' eyes His church is the most beautiful thing in all His glorious, magnificent universe. He desires His church. He yearns for His church.

Jesus is even now preparing His church—in secret. And one day to His church He will come—as a Bridegroom to His bride. To His church He will come—to bestow His Presence in the fullest measure. To His church He will come—to show forth His eternal wisdom and glory to all the principalities and powers in the heavenly places. To His church He will come—to consummate the marriage of Himself and His bride. To His church He will come, and He will bring her into final, complete and everlasting union with Himself—that God may be all in all.

Beloved, let us seek His face. In seeking Him we will find His church—in all her splendor, and in all her beauty. And in finding His church we will find Him—in all His fullness and in all His glory.

Thou, Lord, alone, art all Thy children need,
And there is none beside;
From Thee the streams of blessedness proceed
In Thee the blest abide,—
Fountain of life, and all-abounding grace,
Our source, our center, and our dwelling-place.

CHAPTER EIGHT

The Fullness of Fellowship

And the LORD God formed man of the dust of the ground, and breathed into his nostrils the breath of life; and man became a living soul. (Gen. 2:7)

Man is a unity. God created him in the beginning as a unity. It is a common idea in contemporary theology to view man as being "a spirit, with a soul, in a body". This idea, however, is not Scriptural and it has more basis in Greek philosophy than in the Bible. The Word of God teaches not that man **has** a soul, but that man **is** a soul. The Bible teaches that man is spirit, soul, mind and body. He is one. Each of these integral aspects of his being is as much a part of him as the others.

Man is a unity. God created him as a unity and He intended him to remain as a unity forever. When man sinned he incurred, amongst other things, physical death (i.e. the dissolution of the body, and the separation of the soul, or the person, from the body), and that is why the Gospel of redemption is the Gospel of the resurrection of the body, and the restoration of the unity and wholeness of man.[1]

God created man as a unity, and His original intention was for fellowship with the **whole** man. So when Jesus died to restore man to Himself, He restored **all** of man, and not just one aspect of him (e.g. man's spirit). You have been completely restored to God. Spirit, soul, mind

---

1. 1 Cor. 15

and body, you have been restored to God. God desires that you—all of you—experience His salvation and His fellowship. Do not separate one aspect of your redemption from another. Do not isolate one aspect of your restoration to God from another.

A Complete Restoration to God

Firstly, we have been restored **spiritually** to God. God **is** Spirit, and this is obviously the first and main realm of our fellowship with Him. In fact this is why God originally made man a spiritual being in His image: that man might experience fellowship with Him.

Before we were saved we were spiritually **dead** to God, unable to know Him, unable to love Him. But in the new birth, by a sovereign act of His Spirit, we were made spiritually alive to God, able once again to fellowship with Him, to love Him, to worship Him, and to enjoy Him.

We have been **made alive** to God.[1] And just as a newborn baby needs nourishment and sustenance to grow and develop, so it is with our new spiritual life. Through communion and interaction with God this life is cultivated and developed. Without fellowship with God our new spiritual life will not mature or grow. The new life within us was created in the image of Jesus Christ. Indeed Jesus Himself was the initial Source of this life, and He Himself is its continued Sustenance.[2] In truth, Jesus Himself **is** our life.[3] If He is neglected our inward life will never thrive or flourish.

---

1. Rom. 6:11
2. Col. 3:10; John 4:14; 5:25, 40; 6:33, 57; 14:6
3. John 6:57

Jesus is the true Manna from heaven. You must have Him to live. And just as you need physical refreshment and rejuvenation every day, so you must feed upon the Bread of Heaven daily. Today's "manna" will not be sufficient for tomorrow as well. To live, you must have Him continuously. He is your life. His fellowship is your sustenance.[1] "Man shall not live by bread alone, but by every word that proceedeth out of the mouth of God." To live, you must fellowship with Him daily. You must seek for Him daily. You must cry for Him daily.[2]

We must feed upon Him fresh and anew every day, or else we will become spiritually weak and sickly, and eventually we will expire. As we maintain continuous fellowship with God then we will experience surging spiritual growth and invigoration; and as we come to know Him more and more deeply we will mature as His sons, and by His life within us show forth the light and knowledge of His Unique Son to the world around us.

Furthermore, you have been restored **mentally and intellectually** to God. Do not disregard this. You do not just "have" a mind. You **are** an intellectual being. Your mind has been restored to God. Do not see the mind as something unspiritual or to be despised. In all we have said in a previous chapter about not limiting your relationship with God to a mental exercise, and not substituting mental agreement with doctrine for a true fellowship with God, still know that God wants your mind to be restored to Him. **He** created it in the first place. It is not evil. It is often used for evil purposes, but your mind itself is not intrinsically evil. It was made for good. It was made for **Him.**

God intends your mind to be changed by fellowship with Him. He intends that your mind undergo a process of

---

1. John 6:57
2. Matt. 4:4; John 6:63; Ps. 86:3b

cleansing and transformation. Where once it was blinded and darkened, Jesus Himself wants to be its light. Where once it was "the mind of the flesh", He wants to make it "the mind of Christ". Where once your mind was only an instrument and abode of death, now to you it can be "life and peace". He intends that you use your mind for the furtherance of His glory and your enjoyment of Him. Do not allow your mind to remain unchanged by God, but "be ye transformed by the renewing of your mind".[1]

Without your mind being renewed by God you can have the motivation to do God's will, because of your spiritual regeneration, and yet not know what God's will is. Your life will lack direction and consistency, and you will find yourself carried about by whatever wind of new doctrine blows your way next—whether it be true or false. So give your mind to God. You are an intellectual being. Your intellect is not to be the most important consideration in your life; you are pre-eminently a spiritual being. But you are also an intellectual being, and it was God who made you that way. So do not deny Him access to work in this vital part of you.

Also, you have been restored **emotionally** to God. Do not be afraid of this. Man is an emotional being. You do not just "have" emotions. You **are** an emotional being. **You** have been restored to God. That includes your emotions. Many people are afraid of this, and resist the movings of God upon their hearts when He would seek to touch their emotions. Unfortunately, many Christians see emotions as unspiritual, unnecessary, unstable and unwanted. But they are very important. They are a part of you. They are you. You are emotional. If God touches you then He **will** touch you emotionally.

---

1. 2 Cor. 4:4; 1 Cor. 2:16; Rom. 8:6; 12:2

Without your emotions being renewed by God, you will know what you must do as a Christian, yet it is no joy to you. Your Christian life will be more duty than pleasure. Your need, at this point, is to give God your emotions.

We repeat: do not be afraid of this! Stop letting the fear of man and his opinions rob you of God! Cease ye from man, whose breath is in his nostrils! Allow God to have His way in your life! Let your emotions be moved by Him! Give Him your heart! Give Him your emotions!

Please understand, we are not encouraging you to merely seek after some transient or superficial emotional experience. We are exhorting you to seek God and Him alone. Neither are we advocating that you base your life and your faith upon emotional experiences. You should trust God, and Him alone. The fact is, however, when He touches you, He **will** touch you emotionally, because you **are** emotional—it is that simple.

To deny Jesus access to your emotions is to frustrate His purposes in your life. To deny Him access to your emotions is to deny His Lordship over your life. And to deny Him access to your emotions is to rob yourself of a vital part of the blessing and enjoyment that He intended from all eternity should be yours in Him.

Then, your **will** has been restored to God. Made alive to God, and now indwelt by His Spirit, your will can partake of His glorious life and fellowship. Once bound by self and sin, now your will can be liberated by His life, and enabled to choose **His** perfect will.

Your will must be renewed by God. Without your will being renewed by God, you can understand that something is wrong, be emotionally grieved that you have done it in the past, and yet go right out and do the same thing again! Your need at this point is not necessarily for more teaching, neither is it for more tears. You need God to touch and change your will. You need the life of Jesus to spark and fan a flame of His life within your will, turning it fully towards Himself. Let it be "God who worketh in you both to will and to do of His good pleasure".[1]

Finally, in man's complete restoration to Himself, God did not neglect his body, and one day our **bodily** fellowship with God will be restored. In the eternal state we will see Him and be able to touch and hear Him, just like it was in the time of Adam, who walked and talked **bodily** with the Lord.

While our bodies have been (past tense) redeemed by Jesus' work on the cross, we still have yet to experience the **full manifestation** of that redemption, at which moment we will receive our eternal spiritual bodies.[2] But in the meantime, there is a sense in which our physical bodies do experience His Presence in supernatural healing and Divine health, and a wonderful consequence of restoration to fellowship with God is His daily quickening of our mortal bodies:

> But if the Spirit of Him that raised up Jesus from the dead dwell in you, He that raised up Christ from the dead shall also **quicken your mortal bodies** by His Spirit that dwelleth in you. (Rom. 8:11)

Without your body experiencing the effects of your restoration to God, while your heart may be right with Him, and in a good position to glorify and enjoy Him, yet you will often be too sick to do anything about it! We acknowledge that your spiritual relationship with God can most certainly transcend your own physical dilapidation, and we also recognize that God sometimes will use physical

---

1. Phil. 2:13
2. Rom. 8:23

sickness to correct and chasten.[1] Yet consider that Jesus' provision at the cross for the healing of your body was **His** idea. He made your body for His purposes and glory, and He redeemed it for the same.

So commit your body to the Lord. Jesus is **for** your body. "The body is ... for the Lord; and the Lord for the body ... therefore glorify God in your body, and in your spirit, which are God's". And let God preserve your whole spirit and soul and body, blameless unto the coming of our Lord Jesus Christ.[2]

Here, then, are the blessed effects of the work of Jesus on the cross: the full and complete restoration of man—spirit, soul, mind and body—to God. Be satisfied with nothing less.

---

1. 1 Cor. 5:5; 11:29-31; Ps. 119:67, 71, 75; Matt. 18:35
2. 1 Cor. 6:13, 20; 1 Thess. 5:23

O Thou, to whose all-searching sight
The darkness shineth as the light,
Search, prove my heart; it pants for Thee;
O burst these bonds, and set it free!

Wash out its stains, refine its dross,
Nail my affections to the Cross;
Hallow each thought; let all within
Be clean, as Thou, my Lord, art clean!

(Nicolaus Ludwig von Zinzendorf)

CHAPTER NINE

The Path of Fellowship—the Ministration of Death by the Spirit

> *Now I rejoice, not that ye were made sorry, but that ye sorrowed to repentance ...*
>
> *For godly sorrow worketh repentance to salvation not to be regretted ...*
>
> *... cleanse your hands, ye sinners; and purify your hearts, ye double minded.*
>
> *Be afflicted, and mourn, and weep: let your laughter be turned to mourning, and your joy to heaviness.*
>
> *Humble yourselves in the sight of the Lord, and He shall lift you up. (2 Cor. 7:9-10; Jam. 4:8-10)*

The Holy Spirit is the Spirit of Life. He is God; He is Life. He has come to bring life. Indeed the New covenant is specifically contrasted with the Old as being a ministration of life by the Spirit as over against a ministration of death by the law.[1]

And yet, paradoxically, even under this New Covenant of forgiveness and life, the Holy Spirit has also come to minister death.

This ministration can easily be misunderstood as a negative thing, by those whose Christianity has been reduced to mere theories of positional legalities and judicial standings. Nevertheless, for the Holy Spirit to minister death to the Christian does not imply a contradiction of

---

1. 2 Cor. 3:6-9

what God has made us legally and positionally in Christ, simply because He does not intend to minister death to the New Creation in Christ, but to the old man.

The ministration of death by the Holy Spirit concerns our personal experience: our daily life and walk before the Lord. The ministration of death by the Spirit concerns self, the flesh, the old man.

The biggest enemy of the Christian in his walk with Jesus Christ is not the devil, nor the world, nor even sin: it is **self**. Self is our most dangerous foe. It is to self that Jesus intends to minister death by His Spirit.

God commands us to resist the devil, to flee temptation and to love not the world; but He commands us to **crucify** self—to put it to **death**.

> ... *If any man will come after me, let him deny himself, and take up his cross daily, and follow me. (Luke 9:23)*[1]

Self is our most hideous enemy, our most subtle and deceptive foe. Self is the biggest hindrance to our experiencing the depths of God. It is not just to be resisted, it is not just to be fled, it is not just to be loved not—**self is to be put to death**. Needless to say, the devil, temptation and the attraction of the world are indeed all barriers to God, yet it is **self** that gives them place.

Self is another god before the true God. To choose self is to give allegiance to another god. To assert self is to deny the true God. This is the essence of rebellion and the source of **all** sin: choosing self over God. To know God in truth requires the total renunciation and forsaking of all other gods. Loyalty to none other is accepted before Him. Those who will make up the bride of Christ will stand

---

1. cf. Matt. 10:38; 16:24; Mark 8:34; Luke 14:27

before Him on that Day as "virgins"—free from all unfaithfulness and spiritual defilement—free from all idolatry. Idolatry is to serve another god, whatever it is. The Lord is a jealous God and He has always ministered judgment to all other gods. It is no different with this false god.

To the degree that self is not put to death, we are willingly resisting and **rebelling** against God in our lives. This is true of our lives no matter how religious or spiritual our words and actions may outwardly appear to be. "That which is born of the flesh is flesh; and that which is born of the Spirit is spirit", and "they that are in the flesh cannot please God".

If we are "in the flesh" and yielding to self as the king of our lives, then we are living in rebellion against God. So it is then that we will see the ministration of the Holy Spirit as being destructive, for He is, in truth, seeking to put **us** to death.

As we walk in the Spirit, however, denying self and allowing the Holy Spirit to bring us into union with Christ and His death, then we will see the ministration of the Spirit as being not just the ministration of **death** but the ministration of **life**, for we know by that same Holy Spirit that it is only through the denial of our self that we will experience Him. It is only through experiencing our death that we can ever experience His life. It is only through allowing God to crucify the depths of our self that we will experience His depths.

I am crucified with Christ: nevertheless I live; yet not I, but Christ liveth in me ... (Gal. 2:20)

99

True Life Only Comes Out of Death

Let no man deceive you! The denial and death of self is the only path to enter into the true knowledge of God that He will ever offer you. Wesley's definition of "fanaticism" was: "expecting the end without the means". Try as you may, you **cannot** know God and experience His life without self first being exposed and slain. You **cannot** join Jesus on His throne without first joining Him upon the cross.

The Holy Spirit will **always** attack self. Self is His mortal enemy. The life of the Spirit and the life of self are entirely contradictory and utterly incompatible—they **cannot** co-exist. So when the Holy Spirit moves in a sovereign way upon a church seeking to bring His people into revival and into the depths of experience of Himself, He will **always** move to minister death.

Let us make it clear that the Holy Spirit will move with a clean, sharp sword in these times. It will not be in some vague, ill-defined, generalized castigation that He will come to His people, which thing is more likely to be either a work of the devil or a manifestation of morbid self-absorption than the work of God.

Neither will the effects of this work be depression, disorientation or a lingering discouragement, which again are more likely to be produced by an ungodly brooding and introspection than by Divine inspiration and initiation.

But the Holy Spirit will come quickly, deliberately and specifically; and, with neither fear nor respect of persons, He will pierce right through into the very hearts of His people. Then, exposing His enemy, He will engage with him in mortal combat, until finally the work is complete and His enemy, at least at that particular point, is slain.

It is an historical fact that this precious work of the Holy Spirit will always be opposed and resisted. On the one hand, some will oppose Him out of **ignorance**. Sadly, this number often includes church leaders and preachers, who although declaring that God has called them to bring the people to Himself, rarely understand how God would actually do it; and by their ignorance of the movings of God make themselves worthy targets of the rebuke of Jesus to Nicodemus, "Art thou a teacher of Israel and understandest not these things?"[1]

On the other hand, some will oppose the movings of the Holy Spirit out of **knowledge**.[2] By the inner witness of the Spirit within their own hearts they know that what they see is a work of God, and yet they oppose these special movings of His because they love their life rather than His. While they will always cloak their rebellion in theological terms and point to fleshly abuse and excess within the people embracing the work to discount it, yet at the heart of the matter their opposition to God has exposed them and revealed the true king of their life and the true state of their heart. No matter how religious they may have appeared in the past, they are now exposed as lovers of self rather than lovers of God.

Unfortunately, by resisting death they are paradoxically **choosing** death.[3] They are choosing to abide in death. By resisting destruction they are actually choosing destruction. In saving self they have lost God, and, as Laubach wrote, when "one loses God ... then all is defeat, though it be housed in castles and buried in fortunes".

But those who long for God and consider the personal knowledge of Him worth any price, in these times will yield to the Holy Spirit, submitting their lives to Him, bowing their hearts before Him, exposing their motives, their intents and their innermost purposes and desires to

---

1. 1 Tim. 1:13; John 3:10, Greek
2. John 15:22-24; 1 John 5:10
3. Matt. 10:9

101

His piercing gaze, holding nothing back. Through yielding to the ministration of death by the Spirit, they are making a better and more glorious choice. Those who choose from the bottom of their hearts to yield to the death of self, are in so doing actually choosing **life—His life**.

> *Verily, verily, I say unto you, Except a corn of wheat fall into the ground and die, it abideth alone: but if it die, it bringeth forth much fruit.*
> *He that loveth his life shall lose it; and he that hateth his life in this world shall keep it unto life eternal. (John 12:24-25)*

Let us not find fault with one another in this regard,[1] but let us all examine our own hearts, and face the need for repentance in our own lives. Let us all get down in the dust and seek God with our whole heart for Him to come and sift and slay.

In every one of us, self is very much alive and in the best of health. Self is no weak and sickly invalid. Left to itself it will never die. Self must be deliberately **put to death**. But deaths, and particularly executions, are never pretty sights; and strong men die hard. Consequently, genuine repentance can be quite offensive in the eyes of those who expect religion to be "pleasant" and "inspiring". Nevertheless, when Jesus pronounced the blessing of comfort upon those who mourn, the word He chose for "mourn" literally meant **a grief which is manifested, being too deep for concealment.**[2] So when the Lord is calling His people to repent and mourn and weep and die, then repent and mourn and weep and die!

---

1. 2 Cor. 10:12, 17-18; Gal. 6:3-5
2. Matt. 5:4

When thou saidst, Seek ye my face; my heart said
unto thee, Thy face, LORD, will I seek. (Ps. 27:8)

Do not resist these times, lest you be found even to
fight against God. As Frank Bartleman wrote, these times
are times of "privilege, responsibility and (also) **peril**". Do
not resist His movings. Do not ignore His leadings. Do not
oppose His promptings—not if you want to be known as
one who follows the Lamb whithersoever He goeth. If you
wish Him to know you as one of His own, then do not
rebel against Him in these times.

The Conviction of God Cannot be Worked Up

These movings of the Spirit do not come by the will
of man, but **only** by Divine initiation. If you resist Him,
He may not return in this way for a long time, leaving you
in the barren wilderness of your own fruitless religious
labors. Or, even worse: if you resist Him, He may not
return at all!

So yield to Him. **Yield to Him!**[1] The joy will come
later. There is a time to weep and there is a time to mourn.
The laughter and dancing will come later.[2] Pray it through
now. See it to the end.

At times, because of the depths of self that will be
revealed in your life, it may seem like this work will never
come to an end; but if you will yield to Him, He **will** do
the work. **You will see Him.** He has promised it.[3] So let
Him have His way. Let the Spirit perform His mighty

---

1. see Ps. 32:9
2. Ps. 30:5, 11; Ps. 126:5; Matt. 5:4
3. Matt. 5:8, 6; Phil. 1:6; Heb. 12:14

work. Yield to Him. His Presence is what you are gaining. He Himself is who you are winning.

Someone once said, "All of self, none of God. Less of self, more of God. None of self, all of God." Or, in the words of John the Baptist, "He must increase, but I must decrease." To the extent that your life is ended has His life begun.

The ministration of death by the Holy Spirit is not a desirable thing to those who want only flattery and "smooth words" from God. But it should not be avoided, no matter how painful it may seem for a time. It is one of His most necessary and precious movings on our behalf.[1]

---

1. These times are known as "deeper" experiences to us, and the whole idea of a crucified life is commonly known as the "deeper life". But really we should just call it the "Christian life". It has become the "deeper life" to us because, regrettably, so few of us have ever scratched even the surface of this union with Jesus in His death and life that God has offered us.

CHAPTER TEN

The Requirement for Fellowship— Surrender to God

Who shall ascend into the hill of the LORD? or who shall stand in His holy place?
He that hath clean hands, and a pure heart ...
(Ps. 24:3-4)

Our call is unto God. **He** is the highest and the all encompassing call to the Christian. To know Him is our goal, our ultimate purpose. When we have Him we have **all He is**. We have everything. Salvation, healing, deliverance, eternal security, peace, joy, spiritual strength and power—all are in Him.

When you were saved, God did not intend for you to stop there, but to begin there. When you were born again you were born into His Presence; you were born into union and communion with God, and He wants it to deepen and grow.[1]

But as you seek to grow in your knowledge of God, it soon becomes evident that you have an **enemy** to this pursuit. As we have said, while you can readily identify a number of enemies that are opposed to your going deeper with God, there is one key enemy that opens the door to, and that actually empowers and vitalizes the others. This enemy is not the devil, although he is an enemy; this enemy is not sin, although sin is an enemy; and this enemy

---

1. Col. 1:3; 2 Pet. 1:2-3

is not the world, although the world is an enemy. But your key enemy in the pursuit of God is your own self-will.

The devil **will** keep you from God, but only as **you** give him place. Sin **will** keep you from God, but only as **you** yield to temptation. The world **will** keep you from God, but only as **you** allow it to capture your affections.[1] So the devil, sin and the world are not really the problem. They **become** problems and opposers of God in your life only as **you** allow them to gain a hold in your heart.

Jesus has already stripped Satan of his power, crucified the body of sin, and overcome the world.[2] The enemy that remains to be conquered is self. This is the key to victory in your life, or the source of defeat. Before the devil, sin and the world can be truly dealt with and overcome in your life, you must **first** deal with what gives them power in your life: **self**. Self must be put to death.

Abandonment to God

Self is deeply rooted to the things of this world. By serving the things of this life we are serving and fortifying self. To find God in His fullness self must be crucified, and in that process this world must be abandoned. God requires of us abandonment to Him—abandonment of everything.

You cannot own the field of the Kingdom of God without first giving up **all** we have and **all** we are to buy it.[3] The affection of everything must be forsaken: the world, career, religious position, interests, money, family, things. You can keep nothing. Settle it! The most miserable

---

1. Eph. 4:27; 2 Tim. 2:22; 1 John 2:15-17; Matt. 5:19-21
2. Heb. 2:14-15; Rom. 6:6; John 16:33
3. Matt. 13:44-46

person in the world is a Christian with a divided heart. "Ye **cannot** serve God and mammon."

And what an insult to God it is to offer Him anything less than it all! What a perfect insult to offer Him only half your life, keeping the other half for yourself! He is **GOD!** How can you offer Him anything less than absolute surrender? It is all His anyway. He will take it all to Himself in the end anyway. Ultimately, every knee will bow to Him and confess His Lordship anyway. Ultimately, every life will be to His glory anyway: some will glorify His mercy in their honor and eternal glory, and others will glorify His wrath and power in their dishonor and eternal destruction.[1] But **all** will glorify Him in the end. What foolishness to not freely give all to Him now! He is God. Give Him the only response worthy of Himself: utter absolute abandonment of your entire heart and life to Him.

God wants to be the only Possessor of your life, and the only Possession in your life. And in that position alone is liberty, power, joy, peace, rest and victory.

The man who has abandoned all to God is wholly indestructible. **Nothing** can hurt him. He has already given everything up. He has nothing to lose. Furthermore, in return for the surrender of his life, God has bestowed upon this man **His** life. And the life of God knows neither loss nor defeat! Thus to fully surrender to God is the only path of true victory.

On the other hand, to hold back from God is to secure defeat. "For whosoever will save his life shall lose it".[2] This is why many Christians never really get free from sin, or are continually giving place to Satan, or are constantly being snared in the things of this life: because they have never **fully surrendered** to God. To the extent that you

---

1. Phil. 2:10-11; Rom. 9:21-23
2. Matt. 16:25; cf. 1 Tim. 6:7-10

have surrendered your life to Jesus, forsaking all things, allowing self to be crucified and put to death, is the same extent to which you will walk in victory over all adversaries.

If you will **first** come to a place of surrender to God then the rest will follow. Do not be satisfied trying to merely prune the branches that are offensive to God— branches of sin, worldliness and unbelief—because others will grow in their places. Deal with the branches of the tree at the **root** of the tree. Destroy the tree at its **roots**, and **all** the branches will die. Deal with the tree at its roots. Deal with your life at your heart. "Make the tree good, and its fruit (will be) good".[1] Make the fountain sweet, and its flow will be sweet.

You say, "I wish I could come into more of God but I just cannot seem to give up this besetting sin". But the besetting sin is not your problem. The besetting sin is a branch. Deal with the root. Give up all affection and attachment for that thing from the bottom of your heart, and turn your affection fully toward Jesus, and then God will be able to deliver you.

> But every man is tempted, when he is drawn away of his own lust and enticed. (Jam. 1:14)

If you give in to temptation, the reason for it lies in **you**. **You** need to repent. Your heart needs to be changed.

You say, "I wish I could stop yielding to those temptations, so then I could have more of the Presence of God in my life". But those temptations are not your problem. Yielding to the temptations is a branch. Deal with the root. You yield to the temptations because you still love the sin. The sin is not so much in your outward actions—

---

1. Matt. 12:33; see also Matt. 7:17; 12:34-35; Prov. 4:23b

the sin was in your heart, long before the actions were ever committed. Allow God to deal with your heart and the temptations will no longer have any power. The teeth of the lion will have been pulled.[1]

You say, "I wish I could trust God to fulfill His promises, but there is so much unbelief in my heart". But unbelief probably is not your problem. Unbelief is often a manifestation of a more fundamental problem: you are not surrendered to God. Trusting God for everything He has promised is a simple and natural consequence of having surrendered to God from your heart. Anyone with a clear mind knows that God, as Creator of all things, is **able** to keep all His promises, and is **able** to provide for all your needs—spirit, soul, mind and body. The real question is: have you abandoned yourself to God? Have you surrendered your life, from your heart, into His hands?

He wants you to know Him as the All-Sufficient One, the Provider of all your needs. But you must surrender your life to Him from the bottom of your heart—trusting in Him to meet all of your needs to His glory.

Someone might say, "I believe God moves in response to our **faith**." EXACTLY! And there is only one true faith and that is faith that abides in a surrendered heart.

> ... *but to this man will I look, even to him that is poor and of a contrite spirit, and trembleth at my word. (Is. 66:2b)*

Jesus did not teach faith first. He taught repentance first, and then faith. "Repent ye, and believe the gospel."[2]

---

1. There may also be a need for deliverance from evil spirits. But again, the key to deliverance is unfeigned surrender to God, without which the spirits will continue to have rights of habitation in your life.

2. Mark 1:15; Acts 13:24; 19:4; Matt. 3:11; John 1:31; Luke 1:76; Acts 20:21; Heb. 6:1

Any "gospel" that teaches faith in God without surrender to Him is a false gospel.

This is why some saints who have been dedicated Christians for years can never seem to get healed or delivered by God, in spite of their having heard an abundance of "faith teaching", and in spite of their desire to be healed or delivered and their belief that God can do it; while on the other hand, there are many examples in the New Testament of those who had not even heard an entire discourse by Jesus on **any** subject, and yet when they came to Him they were at once healed or delivered. They received because they came to Him in the simplicity of a yielded heart in faith.

Both repentance and faith are necessary; neither one by itself is enough to receive from God.[1] Effective faith is always that faith accompanied by, and produced by, an abandoned heart. "For the Lord heareth the poor".[2]

The Perils of Knowledge Without Surrender

So we can see that to try to exercise faith without a surrendered heart is destined to failure. Similarly, to approach the Word of God without an abandoned heart is not only an exercise that will fail to produce authentic spiritual fruit but it is downright dangerous as well. As we have said in a previous chapter: as you get into the Word and the Word gets into you it **will** bring you to God, but **only** as you approach it with a surrendered heart.

If you approach God's Word without a surrendered heart one of two things will inevitably happen: either you will reject the Word as invalid, irrelevant or wrong,

---

1. James 1:6-8; 4:3
2. Ps. 69:33a

because it convicts you in an area in which you refuse to yield; or, you will replace the true dealings of God through His Word upon your heart with an academic exercise. That is, you will admire the Word and discuss the Word and analyze the Word and consider what it means **without** really becoming subject to it and applying it to yourself as something **you** need to change on.[1] You place yourself over the Word as **its** divider instead of receiving the Word as **your** divider, and in you the Scripture will be fulfilled: "Ever learning, and never able to come to the knowledge of the truth".[2] For as the body without the spirit is dead, and as faith without works is dead, so head-knowledge without heart-surrender is dead also.

To say the same thing in another way: when you approach the Word of God with an unsurrendered heart you will often intellectually agree with the truth of the Word without becoming subject to its dealings and its attempts to change you. Inwardly you refuse to change, all the time appearing holy and devout, and (horror of horrors!) even **knowledgeable**—often to the point of spiritual pride—about the very Word of Truth that would slay you!

The world seeks for knowledge to gain advancement, honor and esteem in the eyes of other men. Let us never be guilty of this in spiritual matters. If we have this motive, one of the first places it will show up will be in "religious exhibitionism". This is always a give-away. If we possess true spiritual knowledge we will not display it in self-glorifying exhibitions. That is not spiritual knowledge but "worldly knowledge". By "worldly knowledge" we do not mean knowledge necessarily **about** the world, but knowledge **in the manner of** the world. It is merely knowledge about religious matters. It is not true spiritual knowledge.

---

1. Ezek. 33:30-32
2. 2 Tim. 3:7; see also Jam. 1:22; 2:14-26

God never gave us His Holy Word that we should use it for the advancement of our own religious prestige and importance. But self-promotion will inevitably spring from an unsurrendered heart that is instructed in religious matters. Self wants **so much**, and seeks **so tirelessly**, the praise and recognition of men.

Dear brother or sister, if you see this in your life, flee from it. Repent of trying to use the things of God for your own carnal promotion before men. Surrender to Him. Let Him bring you to Himself. He is worth more than the approval and esteem of men! Let His Spirit and His Word do their true work in your life.

If you will surrender to God from your heart, His Word will do a deep exposing work in you, putting self to death and bringing you to God; but you must approach it honestly and sincerely, genuinely prepared to submit to it. It is vain to discuss and debate, or even to agree with the Word of God unless you really are willing to yield to Him who is both its Author and Subject.

The Need for Repentance

There is a further manifestation of religious knowledge without heart surrender that we must recognize. One of the most subtle and most effective ways to hinder a move of God in your life, or in your church, is to misinterpret His dealings as being for the purpose of bringing **others** to repentance and surrender to God. But in a manner of speaking, God is not trying to bring someone else to repentance—He is trying to bring **you** to repentance!

Unfortunately in all of us there is a desire to avoid the cross, while at the same time piously assigning its demands to others and to "the church" as a whole.

But it is **YOU** who need repentance; it is **YOU** who need to surrender and to abandon your life to God; it is

YOU who need the cross. If **YOU** would submit your stubborn heart to God and allow Him to work in your life then God's greatest hindrance to accomplishing His will in the church and bringing His people to a place of reality before Himself would be removed.

Dear brother or sister, if only **one** person in your church would get down and pray it through before God, and come to a place of total surrender to Him—not merely an understanding of this, nor merely a religious profession of it, but the inward reality of a complete abandonment of their life to Jesus—if only one would do this—if God had only one pure instrument, only one channel through whom He could travail and birth a work, then the fire of the Holy Spirit would soon sweep your church and no-one would be left untouched. So let that "one" be you.

It is easy when God begins to deal with you, revealing your own hypocrisy and religious hardness, to immediately see the shallowness of **everyone else's** relationship with Jesus. But you cannot blame others for not yielding to the Holy Spirit. Really the problem is with you, and you just want to point out someone else's hard heart to hide the fact that **your** life is not surrendered to God.

True revival must start somewhere—and it must begin with you. If there is not revival in your church then the fault does not lie in any direction but one.

The problem lies not in your brother;
The problem lies not in your sister.
The problem lies not in the pulpit;
The problem lies not in the pew.

The problem dear brother,
The problem dear sister,

The problem,

The problem

is

you.

One of the most subtle manifestations of self in our lives is to acknowledge the need of repentance and yet to loudly consign that need to everyone but ourselves. And even more awful is the bitter and fault-finding spirit and the censure of others—for their not yielding to God—that frequently accompanies this attitude. All along, self is allowed to hide and take refuge behind this disguise which, amazingly, is the loud and uncompromising proclamation of the need for repentance and death to self! What an extraordinary sight: self fearlessly expounding upon the absolute necessity of death to self! And more incredible yet, in this very process self is actually being defended and even strengthened!

But God has not called you to castigate others over their need for repentance and dying to self. He has called you actually to repent and to die to self—yourself! And without that work in your own life, all of your heated exhortations and admonitions of others will be to no avail, and will probably cause more harm than good.

God does not want self-righteous expositions of everyone else's problem, but your own utter raw abandonment.

It is the same for all Christian exercises. Without this most fundamental of operations—that is the abandonment of the heart to God—all are destined to failure.

There are a myriad of goals and activities pursued by Christians. Yet coming to the knowledge of Jesus Christ is our only true goal, our only real prize. But to come to the knowledge of Jesus **requires** the abandonment of our lives to God.

> *But what things were gain to me, those I counted loss for Christ.*
> *Yea doubtless, and I count all things but loss for the excellency of the knowledge of Christ Jesus my Lord: for whom I have suffered the loss of all things, and do count them but dung, **that I may win Christ** ... That I may know Him (Phil. 3:7-8, 10)*

If our supreme goal is to come to the true knowledge of Jesus then we **must** abandon our lives in entirety to God, and this is why "substitute goals" are so popular: because all of them can be outwardly pursued and an external veneer of Christianity and spirituality fabricated while inwardly **the heart has never surrendered to God and self is still served.**

Religious man is capable of **great** self-deception. We must not rest while even the slightest trace of this appears in our hearts and lives, for the massive iceberg lies beneath. Let us cry day and night to God that He will bring us to Truth.

Jesus, thine all-victorious love
Shed in my heart abroad:
Then shall my feet no longer rove,
Rooted and fix'd in God.

O that in me the sacred fire
Might now begin to glow;
Burn up the dross of base desire,
And make the mountains flow.

O that it now from heaven might fall,
And all my sins consume:
Come, Holy Ghost, for Thee I call;
Spirit of burning, come.

Refining fire, go through my heart;
Illuminate my soul;
Scatter Thy life through every part,
And sanctify the whole.

My steadfast soul, from falling free,
Shall then no longer move;
While Christ is all the world to me,
And all my heart is love.

(Charles Wesley)

CHAPTER ELEVEN

Hindrances to Fellowship

... I dwell in the high and holy place, with him also that is of a contrite and humble spirit ...

For he is not a Jew, which is one outwardly; neither is that circumcision, which is outward in the flesh:

But he is a Jew, which is one inwardly; and circumcision is that of the heart, in the spirit, and not in the letter; whose praise is not from men, but from God. (Is. 57:15; Rom. 2:28-29)

Inasmuch as surrender to God is the entrance, from our side, to fellowship with Him; it follows that any enemy to our surrender to God is an enemy of our fellowship with Him. Self being our chief enemy in this regard; it follows that anything that supports or strengthens self is something to be supremely loathed and most judiciously avoided, for its mission is to accomplish nothing less than the most terrible harm imaginable toward us; that is, to keep us from God. If you would grant this, please grant one thing more: that the culprit most responsible for the advancing of the cause of self, more than any other, is **pride.**

Remember what it was that launched the earliest act of rebellion against God: **self-will fueled by pride.** This was Satan's original sin:

Thine heart was lifted up because of thy beauty, thou hast corrupted thy wisdom by reason of thy brightness: I will cast thee to the ground ...

*For thou hast said in thine heart, I will ascend
into heaven, I will exalt my throne above the stars of
God ...*

*I will ascend above the heights of the clouds; I
will be like the Most High.*

*Yet thou shalt be brought down to hell, to the
sides of the pit. (Ezek. 28:17; Is. 14:13-15)*

Such is the utter futility of self-will, and the supreme
blindness of the pride that incites it. Satan embarked upon
a course of absolute self destruction, that has insanely been
emulated by mankind ever since. What perfect foolishness!
What matchless folly! To refuse to bow the heart to the
superiority of God over oneself, and to the
unchallengeableness of His right to command our unconditional and unquestioning love, allegiance, worship and
obedience, is nothing less than **to choose self-destruction**.

There are Only Two Choices

When He created moral beings with the capacity to
choose, and the right to decide, God permitted the beginning of the great conflict of choice that has raged ever
since, both in the heavens and upon the earth; that is, "I or
Him?"

We say He "permitted" the start of this conflict,
because to give a moral being the reality of choice and the
ability of will, does not of itself necessarily cause any conflict, since there is no conflict at all as long as our choice
is Him. The ability of choice is not wrong in itself. The
existence of will in itself is not evil. It is only when the
wrong choice is made that there is rebellion and sin; and
there is only **one** right choice ever—**HIM**.

God did not give angels or men the ability to choose
for any other reason except that they should freely choose

Him. God's gift of will to men and angels was for one purpose: that they should have the blessed opportunity and glorious privilege of choosing Him. He did not intend that they reject Him. How inconceivable that anyone would! And yet even with the hindsight of many thousands of years of observing the devastating results of making the wrong choice ... man still does it every day!

There are basically only two choices at any time: God or I. This we have identified as the great conflict of the ages, in which all created moral beings participate. When Adam made the first wrong choice on behalf of men, and yielded to self-will instead of the will of God, he died to God, his nature became sinful and corrupt, and his will became bound: bound to self—that is bound to sin—and bound for eternal destruction. All the sons of Adam no matter what their degree of education, wealth, pedigree, or religious training, will **always** make the same choice: self. Man, left to himself, will never choose God—never! His will is bound.

> *Yet man is born unto trouble, as the sparks fly upward. (Job 5:7)[1]*

It is to this pathetic creature that the precious Holy Spirit comes in the new birth, and by an incredible miracle of Divine fiat, He speaks life where there was death, and liberty where there was bondage, restoring once again to man the ability to choose. The Christian thereby becomes a recipient of that great and blessed capacity of being able to choose the will of God.

There is not, and never will be, any more glorious privilege allowed man than this: to freely choose the will of God. Neither is there any greater pleasure that will ever

---

1. see also Eccl. 7:20; Ps. 51:5; 58:3; Rom. 5:12; 3:10

come to man but what comes as a result of freely choosing God's will. To choose His will is to enjoy Him. To choose His will for ever, is to enjoy Him for ever. This is what we were made for. To reject God's will is to reject Him and to hate Him, and it is to choose more of the death and misery that has been man's wretched lot ever since Adam's Fall.

We were not created to reject God. We were created to obey Him, and to enjoy Him for ever. To choose the will of God is nothing less than to love Him and is nothing less than to choose life. His will is our life and our love of Him. It is all the same: to love Him is to do His will, is to allow His life to spring up inside us and through us, is to love Him and is to participate in His love for us. "To live is Christ". This is our calling. This is our enjoyment of Him. This is our fellowship with Him. This is our union with Him. This is our participation in His life. This is to abide in Him and He in us. This is the life "hid with Christ in God".

On the other hand, as the Christian is free to do the will of God, so he is also assuredly free to continue to choose self, just as he has done all his life prior to conversion. But those who consistently make this choice, without contrition or repentance, and tread under foot the Son of God whose sacrifice made possible our salvation from self, sin and destruction, are spoken of in the New Testament with a severity that is not parallelled in the entire Bible:

> *For it is impossible ... if they shall fall away, to renew them again unto repentance; seeing they crucify to themselves the Son of God afresh, and put Him to an open shame.*
>
> *But it is happened unto them according to the true proverb, The dog is turned to his own vomit again; and the sow that was washed to her wallowing in the mire.*

For if we sin wilfully, after that we have received the knowledge of the truth, there remaineth no more sacrifice for sins,

But a certain fearful looking for of judgment and fiery indignation, which shall devour the adversaries.

But that which beareth thorns and briers is rejected, and is nigh unto cursing; whose end is to be burned. (Heb. 6:4, 6; 2 Pet. 2:22; Heb. 10:26-27; 6:8)[1]

Now remember, it is not the outward religiosity of one's words or works that means you are necessarily walking with God, but the fact of the inward choosing of the will of God over the will of self, and the reality of the life and fellowship of God abiding within you.

Needless to say, those who are living in outward sin and rebellion cannot make any claim to eternal life,[2] but neither can those who **in their hearts** have not yielded their lives to God, no matter how outwardly righteous they may appear to be.

Tragically, many professing Christians think they are saved and in right-standing with God merely on the grounds of an external identification with Christianity or with some doctrine or church. Their awakening to their true condition before God, on the last day, will be rude indeed:

Not every one that saith unto me, Lord, Lord, shall enter into the kingdom of heaven; but he that doeth the will of my Father which is in heaven.

Many will say to me in that day, Lord, Lord, have we not prophesied in thy name? and in thy name have

---

1. see also Matt. 24:48-51; 1 Jn. 5:16
2. Eph. 5:5-7; 1 Cor. 6:9-10; Gal. 5:19-21

cast out devils? and in thy name done many wonderful works?

*And then will I profess unto them, **I never knew you**: depart from me, ye that work iniquity. (Matt. 7:21-23)*

Your outward religious appearance is not what will count before Jesus on the last day. Only one thing is acceptable to God and that is inward surrender and yielding to Him; and without that, even your most righteous words and works are as filthy rags in His sight. Without His life living in and through you, you can do nothing but what is sin in His eyes.[1]

The rich young ruler in the Gospels lived a life of complete obedience to what he had been taught from God's Word.[2] He thought he had kept all of its commandments from his youth up. His life, in the eyes of other men, was righteous and godly, surely deserving of God's warmest approval. Yet Jesus said that the young man lacked "one thing", and that this one thing was so indispensable that its lack would prevent the man from entering into the eternal Kingdom of God. The one thing he lacked was abandonment to God. The one thing he lacked was the complete surrender of his life—with all it included—from his heart, to God. And the lack of that **one** thing kept this man from eternal life, irrespective of the myriad of works of outward righteousness that he had accomplished in his lifetime.

Dear friend, abandon yourself to God! Do not deceive yourself that you are right with God and heading towards heaven as your eternal home, without having entirely surrendered your life to Jesus. Jesus must be **Lord** in reality, not just in word.

---

1. Is. 64:6; John 15:4-5
2. Luke 18:18-25

But this is where pride comes in, and this is where the snare of man's religion enters. Pride is so extremely subtle and religion is such a powerful ally, that self in its effort to stay alive and in control of your life, turns to them for assistance. Rather than submit to denial and crucifixion, self becomes religious and adopts the outward forms of piety and spirituality, while not at all yielding to the inward workings of God, and not at all lovingly obeying Him in truth. In this way an outward appearance of Truth is constructed, while inwardly, the heart has never surrendered to God.[1]

Vigorously buttressed and defended by self-justifying pride, this religious facade is thus a difficult fortress to penetrate, and it resists all but the most powerful battering rams of the movings of the Holy Spirit. It cannot be argued or reasoned into surrender. Indeed it will agree wholeheartedly with every religious discourse, all the while never yielding one inch to God.

Consider the chief priests and scribes of Herod's time, who knew the Word of God well enough to be able to direct the wise men from the East to the birth place of the Messiah, and yet never travelled the road themselves to bow at His feet! In the eyes of men they were recognized as knowledgeable religious leaders, but in their hearts they did not want to know God, or to surrender to the One "that shall **rule** my people Israel", and so they never sought Him. When they eventually did see Him, after He came to them, they not only "received Him not"—they **hated** Him, and closed their ears and eyes against Him, absolutely rejecting Him. "We **will not** have this Man to reign over us."[2]

---

1. see Matt. 23:25-28
2. Matt. 2:1-6; Luke 19:14; Matt. 13:15; John 5:40; 1:11; 15:24; 3:20; Is. 53:3; Acts 28:27

Likewise, Pilate beheld Truth Himself, and yet reduced the experience to debate and philosophical questionings, "What is truth?" He **professed** to be seeking Truth, yet obviously not sincerely.

Or consider Saul, who, prior to his conversion, was brought up at the feet of the renowned teacher of the Word, Gamaliel, and was "taught according to the perfect manner of the law of the fathers". Saul was a "Hebrew of the Hebrews; as touching the law, a Pharisee ... touching the righteousness which is in the law, blameless".[1] And yet he fiercely persecuted the followers of the very God of his beloved law, and when he finally encountered God Himself, **about whom** he had studied all his life, his response was "Who art thou, Lord?".[2]

Remember the people who Jesus came to, and who utterly rejected Him. It was Israel—God's own chosen nation—the only people on the face of the earth with the true revelation of God's Word.[3] Israel "had the Word" in outward appearance, but not in inward reality.

Some of the most outwardly pious people of His day, Jesus called "liars", "murderers" and "children of the devil"! These men, Jesus said, "outwardly appear righteous unto men, but within ... are full of hypocrisy and iniquity."[4] These were the spiritual leaders of that day— the finest the religious community had to offer. Outwardly they had conformed to the accepted religious standards of their time and place, but inwardly they had never yielded to God. Externally they had adopted all the right habits, and codes of dress, and manners of speaking, but in their hearts they had never abandoned self for the will of God.

---

1. Acts 22:3; Phil. 3:5-6
2. Acts 9:5
3. Ps. 147:19-20
4. Matt. 23; John 8

They knew the Word of God and were even able to teach it to others,[1] yet God they knew not. They commanded others to obey the Word of God, but when God **Himself** came to them they utterly rejected Him.

> *Ye hypocrites, well did Isaiah prophesy of you, saying, This people draweth nigh unto me with their mouth, and honoureth me with their lips; but their heart is far from me. (Matt. 15:7-8)*[2]

These men, the spiritual authorities of their generation, had never submitted to God. They had never been truly changed. They were not choosing the will of God. They did not love God. They did not know God. They had never come into fellowship with God. They were not saved. They were not right with God. Yet here is the deception: **they thought they were!**

Religious self-deception is the most awful form of deception possible, and the **hardest** for many people to be set free from—chiefly, because deep in their hearts **they want it and have actually chosen it!**

Has this taken place in your life, dear Christian? To any degree? The tell-tale sign of this most awful state of falling away from God is not an outward forsaking of religion—not by any means! It is the inward lack of the Presence and the fellowship of God in your life.

In Exodus chapter thirty-three, in response to Israel's sin and pride, God had Moses take the tabernacle, the place of His dwelling, and remove it from the midst of His people, setting it up "afar off" from the camp.[3] Think on this: a people that bore the name of the true God in the

---

1. Matt. 23:1-3
2. see also Ps. 78:36-37; Ezek. 33:31-32
3. Acts 7:39; Ex. 33:3, 7

midst of a world filled with idols and false gods; a people that continued to experience the provision of God by the supernatural supply of food from heaven and drink from the rocks; a people just recently supernaturally delivered from the hands of their enemies through the split Red Sea; a people that enjoyed the miraculous protection and guidance of God by the pillar of cloud by day and the pillar of fire by night; a people who left a life of slavery in Egypt without even a single feeble person among all their tribes; a people that had beheld the very words of God written with the finger of God on the tables of stone; a people that dwelt with the meekest man upon the face of the earth, and a prophet so great that the Messiah was said to be a Prophet like unto him; a people who had seen the awesome works and splendor of the Creator; a people with all the outward signs of being right with God—**yet a people whose God dwelt afar off!**

Dear brother or sister, the proof of your faith does not lie in the fact that you are called by the name of "Christian".[1] Neither does it lie in the fact that you may be well taught in the Word of God;[2] or because you can quote the promises of God; or because you seem to dwell at ease and in comfort; or because you see a miracle or healing every now and then; or because you identify with a spiritual church or movement; or because you prophesy or feed the poor; or because you have sat under the ministry of a great man of God; or because you are well-read in, and approve of, the experiences of other great saints of God.

Take no comfort in any of these things, "for I say unto you, that God is able of these stones to raise up

---

1. Rev. 3:1
2. see Rom. 2:17-23

children unto Abraham".[1] Your only true certainty of eternal life lies in the reality of your daily submission and yielding to Jesus Christ as the Lord and God of your life, and the object of your love and inward communion. As Finney said, it is the "state of entire and universal devotion to God which constitutes true religion". The evidence of salvation is not religious outward works, but inward abandonment to God and the experience of loving fellowship with Him.[2]

The great hindrance to fellowship with God in your life is self-will, the great energizer of self-will is pride, and the great cloak of them both is man's religion.

---

1. Matt. 3:9
2. Of course this will, in turn, produce acceptable works of righteousness.

Content with beholding His face,
My all to His pleasure resign'd,
No changes of season or place
Would make any change in my mind:
While blest with a sense of His love,
A palace a toy would appear;
And prisons would palaces prove,
If Jesus would dwell with me there.

(John Newton)

CHAPTER TWELVE

The Imperative of Fellowship

*Whom having not seen, ye love; in whom, though
now ye see Him not, yet believing, ye rejoice with joy
unspeakable and full of glory ... (1 Pet. 1:8)*

This life is fundamentally not a time of ultimate reward,
but it is a time of probation, trial and testing.[1] We do not
enjoy our consummate crown here in this life, but in
eternity.

We will finally rest and be at peace in eternity. Here
we rest in the midst of the battle. Here we are at peace in
the midst of the storm.[2]

In the same way, the **fullness** of our knowledge of
God will not be experienced on this side of the veil.

*For now we see through a glass, darkly; but then
face to face: now I know in part; but then shall I know
even as also I am known. (1 Cor. 13:12)*

We will only come to our fullest knowledge of Christ
in the next life—whether after death or the rapture. In this
life we can only possess the "firstfruits of the Spirit". The
fullness is to come.[3]

---

1. Job 7:17-18; Ps. 66:10
2. John 17:15; 16:33
3. John 14:3; 2 Cor. 5:6-8; Phil. 1:23; 1 Thess. 4:17; 5:10; Rom. 8:23

The truth remains, however, of the great promise of God that constitutes the Christian life; namely, that we love and enjoy Him, and He loves and enjoys us, **NOW**, as well as in eternity. It is a central part of God's plan that we **do** experience and know Him here and now. Indeed it will **only** be through our fellowship with Jesus that we will overcome in the trials and testings now anyway.

God does not allow the trials of this life to see if we can overcome them **without** Him, but that we might overcome them **with** Him. Our sufferings in this life— through temptation, trial, persecution and affliction—are not to be endured apart from God, but they are to be overcome **through** and **in** Him. Only then will they be eternally beneficial to us.

There is a certain work that can **only** be accomplished in us during this life. There is no suffering in the eternal state of the righteous. Neither is there pain. Neither are there unanswered questions. There is no temptation, sin nor devil in the New Jerusalem. Neither is there self-will nor rebellion. Neither is there church division, misunderstanding nor strife. Those things are only obstacles to us here and now—in this life. So although we most definitely will be learning and increasing in our knowledge of God throughout eternity, yet our only chance to conquer those particular adversaries is **in this life.**

The Necessity of Sufferings

We can identify a twofold purpose of our sufferings in this life: one purpose is toward man, and the other is toward God. Toward man, our sufferings enable us to empathize with suffering humanity. Consider God Himself: although He **is** perfect and infinite Love from eternity, yet He had to take upon Himself human nature to be able to suffer and to be tempted as a man, which experiences in turn have enabled Him to "succour" and to "have compassion on" frail humanity.[1] Could it be any different with us? Although our hearts may be full of love and pity for the people around us, yet until we ourselves have personally experienced the sufferings they undergo, we can never really understand their condition or truly empathize with them. If we lack concern for the terrible plight of those around us, it may not necessarily reflect a lack of "love" on our part, but merely our lack of the experience of like sufferings; hence the **necessity** of our sufferings.

Furthermore, as we turn our hearts fully toward God to obtain His strength in time of suffering, and do actually **receive** from Him comfort and strength, we will accordingly have a store of spiritual comfort and power out of which we can give to others in their times of need. "So then death worketh in us, but life in you."[2] It is only when death is really working in us that the life of Jesus will flow out of us to others. If we have never received this kind of comfort from God in our own times of adversity, however, it would be a vain thing to try to minister it to others. We can only give to someone what we ourselves have first received. So it is clearly evident that without union with Christ in His sufferings, God can never use us for the fullest blessing of others—and that in spite of all the religious proficiency and expertise we may possess.

So let us be willing to put ourselves in His hands, where He will break us like the five barley loaves. Remember, it was only **after** Jesus had broken the bread— that He could distribute it to feed the multitude.

Then, toward God, our sufferings give us an opportunity to "learn obedience" to our Heavenly Father in a way we could otherwise never have. It is easy to obey God

---

1. Heb. 2:18; 4:15; 5:1-2
2. see 2 Cor. 1:4; 4:12

when things are going our way; but when persecution arises for the sake of the Word and of righteousness, then we have our first chance to practise the devotion and obedience to God we have previously declared.

It is easy to say we love God for Himself when everything is working out. But what if it will cost us everything—our own goals and ambitions and comforts, even our own lives—to serve Him? Will we still love Him for His own sake?

Likewise, it is easy to say we trust God to meet all our needs when we have no need above our own ability to satisfy. It is only through times of difficulty, sickness, misunderstanding or hardship that we have the chance to **prove** our faith.

Again, it is easy to boldly—and ever so piously— declare our theoretical willingness to die as martyrs for the Lord. But how loudly do we thank Him when He gives us the chance to die, not just once but **daily**—to our own desires, views, ideas, and feelings—on behalf of our brothers and sisters in Christ?

So we see that our sufferings, trials and adversities give us **opportunities** to be faithful to God; and without these opportunities, our faithfulness—or lack of it—can never be revealed.

Muscles need resistance to grow strong. And it is only after it has begun to hurt that anything is being built. Dead wood beneath the earth needs **great** pressure to be transformed into coal which is useful. And with even more pressure diamonds can be formed. In the same way, our spiritual character must have opposition and resistance for it to mature. Pain must be experienced. Pressure must be endured. "No conflict, no character." "Without strife, a weak life." It is through overcoming temptation and trial that we grow spiritually strong. It is through suffering, in all its forms, that we have the opportunity to learn obedience to God and to be perfected by Him. Thus our trials and sufferings mature us, making us perfect and complete before God, and partakers of His glory.[1]

But trials and sufferings not only **perfect** some Christians—they also **destroy** some others. The same fire that tempers the blade of the sword also melts and consumes other metals. The pressure within the ground that transforms some wood into coal that will brightly burn as a testimony to the Author of its transformation, also crushes other wood into dust.

> *And whosoever shall fall on this stone shall be broken: but on whomsoever it shall fall, it will grind him to powder. (Matt. 21:44)*

So it is not the suffering itself that transforms or destroys us: it is our response to it that does the work. Your sufferings will only be instruments of your transformation and perfection if you respond to them the right way. If you run from them; in self-pity complain bitterly about them; do all you can to avoid them, and thus despise them; then you have disregarded a major purpose of this life.

God's intention in allowing the trial is that you abandon all hope and trust in your own strength, and in your own ways, and in the things of this life to sustain you, and throw yourself more completely upon Jesus and His wonderful grace. If you will, in this way, submit yourself to your faithful Creator, rejoicing in whatever He allows to come your way, knowing it is all for your ultimate greater participation in His glory, then you will have learned the meaning of your life upon the earth.

You also will have begun to understand the answer to the great mystery of why God did not cast Lucifer into the

---

1. cf. Heb. 2:10-11; 5:8-9. If the Son of God Himself was made mature through His sufferings, how could it be any other way with us?

eternal lake of fire the moment he first rebelled,[1] as well
as why God did not take you to your eternal home in glory
the moment you were saved. This life is indeed brief, but
it has a profound meaning. So accept the fact that God's
purpose in this life is not your temporal comfort and
blessing, but your eternal transformation and His eternal
glory. Your life on this earth is the foundation of your life
in eternity. View your trials and sufferings in this light,
and you will recognize they are not working **against** you to
destroy you, but they are working **for** you, to perfect you.

*For our light affliction, which is but for a
moment, **worketh for us** a far more exceeding and
eternal weight of glory;*
* **While** we look not at the things which are seen,
but at the things which are not seen: for the things
which are seen are temporal; but the things which are
not seen are eternal. (2 Cor. 4:17-18)*

Your sufferings work for you **because** God is for you,
and He is in control over all things. He is the Great
Architect of your life and times, most especially including
your sufferings. Always remember: God is **for** you. He has
already demonstrated the reality and extent of His love for
you in giving you Himself. What greater love could there
be, and what further proof do you need of His love? And
because God is for you, therefore all the circumstances that
He allows, in one way or another, are **for** you—as **long as**
you respond to them the right way.[2]

---

1. The answer is that the devil is merely an instrument in the hands
of our Sovereign God—to fulfill His purposes (Prov. 16:4). When God
is finally finished with the devil, He will then put him away—forever.
    2. Rom. 8:28-39

So do not waste your tests and trials by failing them! Do not squander your temptations by yielding to them! Do not misuse your sufferings and persecutions by stumbling at them! Do not mishandle your afflictions by murmuring and complaining about them! Learn to be obedient through your sufferings. Be made "perfect"—complete and mature —through your sufferings. There will be no opportunity to overcome on the other side of the veil—**for ever!** The depth of maturity that you reach in this life by overcoming temptation and adversity through Christ, and by learning obedience during your sufferings, will be yours eternally. Once this life is over, you will never again have the chance to go deeper with God, at least in this regard.

So submit yourself to God. The vitally important thing in your times of suffering is **not** that you have all your questions answered,[1] but that you submit yourself to God. He does not have to explain your sufferings to you. He wants you to trust Him. The "whys" are not important.[2] In fact, there are even times when it would be more detrimental to your eternal transformation to have all your questions answered than that they should, for the moment, go unanswered.

So trust Him. Trust Him without explanation. Trust Him no matter what He allows.[3] Be assured that He has arranged your circumstances according to His perfect and infinite wisdom. You may not be able to understand all things now, but when you finally stand upon His holy

---

1. Neither is the most important thing that you necessarily get delivered from the suffering. In fact there are times when God may actually **refuse** to deliver you for a season (2 Cor. 12:7-9; Matt. 26:39-42)!

2. Unless, of course, the source of your suffering in a particular instance is the **chastening** hand of your loving Heavenly Father, in which case He naturally wants you to understand the reason for it.

3. Job 13:15a

mountain and look upon the great expanse of your life—indeed upon the vast panorama of all of human history—you will praise and extol the One who, in infinite wisdom, wove such a magnificent and perfectly designed tapestry; the One who, in supreme love, pieced together such a grand and intricate mosaic.

Everything is in His hands. He reigneth over all. And aren't you glad He does? For if it was up to you to govern the affairs of this world and of men—and especially your own affairs—surely you would make a great muddle!

But Jesus is perfect and His government is perfect. He alone is able to make all things work together for good to those who love Him. And so put your trust in Him; knowing that He loves you with an everlasting love; knowing that you are safe in the shadow of His wings; knowing that it will be but a short moment until you will see Him face to lovely face—finally beholding the beauty of the One you have loved; finally to fall before Him and wash those precious nail-scarred feet with your tears.

In that moment of transition, in that brief instant of moving from this world to that eternal one, you will understand why He allowed the things He did upon this earth. For now we see through a glass darkly; but then face to face: now we know in part; but then shall we know even as also we are known. One look at that lovely face, one look into those eyes, those "pools of living love", will far outweigh the power of a million words of explanation for the things of this life. "It will be worth it all when we see Jesus."

What a moment that will be. And what a great revelation. How we will rejoice and shout! How we will leap and dance! In that instant, when the veil has fallen from our eyes, we will see how **perfectly** He did govern His world. From that vantage point we will see the whole spiritual landscape at once, every detail appearing in its proper God-ordained relation to every other one. We will understand how compassionately and how wisely He directed His universe. We shall see how wonderfully He made **all** things work together for our good and for His glory.

Truly He shall wipe away all tears by that revelation. We shall rejoice when we realize that by His grace we did not give up when the most negative of things happened. How grateful we will be that even though things took place that we could not understand, things that did not make sense to our short-sighted intellect, yet we did not give in to discouragement or self-pity but we lifted up the hands that hung down and, strengthening the feeble knees, we committed our lives afresh unto our most faithful Creator, and bowed our shoulders once more to the plow He gave us.

How grateful we will be that by His grace upon our lives we let all things draw us closer to Him, and that through the moving of His Holy Spirit upon our hearts we allowed **nothing** to separate us from His enduring love. How glad we will be that in the most difficult and the most anguishing of times, we turned our hearts completely towards **Him** to love Him and to know Him even more fully, and to worship the One who reigns in the heavens and upon the earth; who controls the hearts and affairs and lives of all men; who does, and does perfectly, what **He** wants in the hosts of heaven, and among the inhabitants of the earth.

What a great thing it is to be a Christian! What a marvelous thing to know that our Heavenly Father loves us and cares for us with an infinite concern. That every hair on our head He has numbered. That, without exception, there are **no** accidents with Him. That every step we take is ordered by Him. That His love for us all is an everlasting one.

Trust Him. He is perfect in wisdom, and He is unconditional in His love toward you. Draw near to Him now. Let Him hold your hand and take you through it all. Trust Him without explanation. Say with Jesus, "the cup which my Father hath given me, shall I not drink it?"[1] Endure your Divinely-appointed sufferings without questionings and murmurings, leaning upon His faithful arm to sustain you. And then, when it is all finished, you will behold, with delight, the grandeur and the glory of the work that you allowed Him to accomplish in you.[2]

As we have said, this is part of the meaning of this life, and it is why it is imperative to draw near to Jesus now and not to just leave the initiation of your relationship with Him to the next life.

> *For our light affliction, which is but for a moment, worketh for us a far more exceeding and eternal weight of glory ...*
>
> *And if children, then heirs; heirs of God, and joint-heirs with Christ; if so be that we suffer with Him, that we may be also glorified together. (2 Cor. 4:17; Rom. 8:17)*

If We Suffer with Him, We shall also Reign with Him

Most Christians know that there are differing degrees of reward for the righteous in eternity.[3] But as hard a saying as this may be to those who dwell in self-contented comfort and ease in Zion, it is also largely true that the measure of our eternal glory with Jesus will be determined, not by the blessings we have received in this life, nor by the religious expertise we have achieved, but by the

---

1. John 18:11
2. 1 Pet. 1:7
3. 1 Cor. 15:41-42; Heb. 11:35

sufferings with Jesus we have experienced while on this earth.

Those who walk with Jesus Christ **will** suffer.[1] Those who will reign with Jesus on His throne for eternity will have suffered greatly.[2] Those who will deeply know Jesus will have deeply known His sufferings. Those who will experience the power of His ascended glory will first have endured the weight of His suffering that preceded it.[3]

God's way has always been the way of conflict and anguish. His path has always led first to the scourging post and then to the cross.

That I may know Him, and the power of His resurrection, and the fellowship of His sufferings, being made conformable unto His death ... (Phil. 3:10)

If you do not know of the sufferings about which we speak, it may be that you have not yet begun to walk closely with your Lord. But if you will set your face to seek Him and to come into His Presence, then you will find that holy Presence leads you, not only into great and unspeakable joy, glory and splendor, but also into a dark shadow of sufferings under His cross. Yet fear not, for in that shadow you will not be left alone. And it will be in that shadow that you will come to experience Christ in all His fullness.

---

1. Acts 14:22; John 15:18-20; Phil. 1:29; 2 Tim. 2:12; 3:12; 1 Thess. 3:3-4; 2 Thess. 1:4-5; 1 Pet. 5:10; Rev. 2:10; Matt. 5:10-12
2. see Matt. 20:20-22
3. 1 Pet. 1:11; 4:12-13

*Yea, though I walk through the valley of the shadow of death, I will fear no evil: for **thou art with me**; thy rod and thy staff they comfort me. (Ps. 23:4)*

Unlike fickle human relationships, which so often are easily dissipated in times of trouble, our relationship with Jesus will endure all things. He is "a friend that sticketh closer than a brother". He will be with you always—even, or should I say **especially**, in times of extremity. "I will **never** leave thee, nor forsake thee."[1] You will discover the Lord is not only God of the hills, but He is God of the valleys.

Furthermore, it is in the very hour of suffering that His Presence should be the most immediate to you.

*... knowing, that as ye are partakers of the suffering, **so shall ye be also of the consolation**. (2 Cor. 1:7)*

In all our sufferings, we suffer **with** Jesus;[2] and not just in the sense that we share the same sufferings He suffered, but more than that. We suffer **with** Him. He is **with** us, manifesting Himself to us, when we suffer.[3] Many are the testimonies through the centuries of saints who were cruelly imprisoned, beaten, tortured, scourged, and burnt alive—who in the midst of it all experienced such a depth of God that in Him even the physical pain was annulled.

Likewise, Jesus on the cross, in His time of greatest trial and suffering, experienced the fellowship of His

---

1. Prov. 18:24; Heb. 13:5c; see also Ps. 46:1
2. Rom. 8:17; Is. 63:9
3. Acts 7:55-56; 9:4-5; 23:11; 26:21-22

Father. He was not separated from His Father while hanging upon the cross, but He knew His Presence:

> *For David speaketh concerning Him (i.e. Jesus on the cross), I foresaw the Lord **always before my face**, for **He is on my right hand**, that I should not be moved ... (Acts 2:25)[1]*

When Jesus, in Mark 15:34, cried, "My God, my God, why hast thou forsaken me?", the meaning of the utterance was not that there was a termination, even for the briefest moment, of His inward fellowship with His Father. The words simply mean that the Father had to **let** His Son die. The Father was **allowing** His Son to suffer and die at the hands of sinful men, to pay the penalty for man's sins. He was "forsaken" **in that sense**.

Jesus was perfect and righteous and, unless the Father deliberately allowed Him to, could not have suffered and died. That was the nature of the forsaking: a forsaking by God of His Son in the sense that He allowed Him to go through circumstances He otherwise would not have experienced, circumstances from which the Father would otherwise have delivered His righteous Son. Jesus' words did not at all imply a severing of His spiritual relationship and inward communion with His Father. He was always in fellowship with His Father. "I have set the Lord always before me". Throughout the time of the crucifixion, the Father was with Jesus, upholding and strengthening Him: "He is on my right hand, that I should not be moved."[2]

On the cross Jesus did endure the "contradiction of sinners against Himself"—and the anguish of an apparent

---

1. see also Ps. 22:24; John 16:32; 8:28-29; 2 Cor. 5:19
2. Ps. 16: 8; Acts 2:25; see also Luke 23:34, 46; Ps. 22:19; Is. 50:6-9

giving over by God into the hands of undeserved adversity[1]—but He did not experience the loss of His Father's inward fellowship at any time.[2]

Even so in our lives, there are times when it would **appear** that God has forsaken us, when He allows us to go through trials and circumstances that many assume God would deliver His righteous servants from. Others may think God has left us in these times.[3] But this "forsaking" is only apparent and "circumstantial". Inwardly, our spiritual fellowship with our Heavenly Father should not suffer one iota; in fact it should be enhanced.

Our times of trial and suffering should not be experienced apart from God, and it should not be thought that He expects this of us. If His commandment is that we be strong **in the Lord** and in the power of **His** might, and that we do all things through **Christ** who strengthens us, overcoming only in **His** strength, then how is it that we assume He leaves us in times of trial and suffering?

The trial itself does not consist, as many unfortunately think it does, in God's removal of His inward fellowship with us. **The trial involves the disturbing of the outward circumstances and things of this life—not of our inward fellowship with God.** The trial involves the troubling of the feelings of **the five physical senses,** but **not** of our inward consciousness of His fellowship. Outward sufferings and afflictions are not able to disturb the soul that is nestled in the palm of His hand.[4] God is still with us all along, and in the midst of suffering, our inward communion with

---

1. Heb. 12:3; see also Is. 53:4b
2. For a detailed consideration of this question, and of the cross in general, please see our book, "The Precious Blood of the Lord Jesus Christ".
3. Ps. 42:3; 71:11
4. Matt. 10:28; Ps. 57:1; Ps. 91

Him is retained and, now free from outward distraction and attachment, can even blossom and flourish.

> *For as the sufferings of Christ abound in us, so our consolation also **aboundeth** by Christ.*
>
> *Always bearing about in the body the dying of the Lord Jesus, that the **life** also of Jesus might be made manifest in our body. For we which live are alway delivered unto death for Jesus' sake, that the **life** also of Jesus might be made manifest in our mortal flesh.*
>
> *For which cause we faint not; but though our outward man perish, yet the inward man is **renewed** day by day.*
>
> *... I am **filled with comfort**, I am **exceeding joyful** in all our tribulation.*
>
> *If ye be reproached for the Name of Christ, blessed are ye; **for the Spirit of glory and of God resteth upon you** ... (2 Cor. 1:5; 4:10-11, 16; 7:4b; 1 Pet. 4:14)*

Through His fellowship, Jesus enables us to partake of the afflictions of the Gospel, not according to our own strength, but "according to the power of God".[1]

> *Notwithstanding the Lord stood **with me**, and **strengthened** me ... And the Lord shall deliver me from every evil work, and will preserve me unto His heavenly kingdom ... (2 Tim. 4:17-18)*

We obviously are not saying that if you walk with Jesus then you will not have any more trials or sufferings. The truth is, those who are closest to the Lord will be trusted with the **greatest** tests, because, in His strength,

---

1. 2 Tim. 1:8

they are the strongest.[1] What we are saying is that in the
midst of the trial, whatever its nature, your inward
fellowship with God will not dissolve, but it will deepen,
and it will be this inward experience of His Presence and
fellowship that will be your strength in the midst of the
battle, your courage in the midst of alarm, your peace in
the midst of the storm and your victory in the midst of
apparent defeat.

Perhaps you think that God has removed His Presence
from you in times of trial because you equate His Presence
with excitement, "tingles", emotional feelings, "goose-
bumps" and the serenity of your circumstances. So when
outward circumstances turn sour and the feelings turn bad,
you think you have lost God's Presence. But this may only
be indicative of how little you knew of His true Presence
in the first place. Had you previously cultivated a true
inward communion with Jesus you would not in time of
trial think you now experienced the loss of His Presence.
Indeed in these times your awareness of His fellowship
should be refined.

We repeat, Jesus does not command us to forsake our
own self-confidence and strength, only to abandon us to it
again in times of testing. In Him, **in inward fellowship
and communion with Him**, is our only strength and
resource—at all times.

> *I can do all things **through Christ** which
> strengtheneth me.*
> *... in all these things we are more than conquer-
> ors **through Him** that loved us.*
> *Now thanks be unto God, which always causeth us
> to triumph **in Christ** ...*
> *The LORD God is **my strength** ...*

---

1. 1 Cor. 10:13; Matt. 20:20-23

I will go in the strength of the LORD God ...

... God is the strength of my heart ...

... the LORD is the strength of my life; of whom shall I be afraid?

Wait on the LORD ... and He shall strengthen thine heart ... (Phil. 4:13; Rom. 8:37; 2 Cor. 2:14a; Hab. 3:19; Ps. 71:16; 73:26; 27:1, 14)

When circumstances are bad, and in our own strength we are weak and insufficient, those are the very times when the power of God can be made most manifest in our lives if we will surrender and yield to Him:

And He said unto me, My grace is sufficient for thee: for my strength is made perfect in weakness. Most gladly therefore will I rather glory in my weaknesses, that the power of Christ may rest upon me.

Therefore I take pleasure in weaknesses, in reproaches, in necessities, in persecutions, in distresses for Christ's sake; for when I am weak, then am I strong.

... For we also are weak in Him, but we shall live with Him by the power of God ...

... we have this treasure in earthen vessels, that the excellency of the power may be of God, and not of us. (2 Cor. 12:9-10; 13:4b; 4:7)

In the eyes of man, weakness is disdained, and those who are weak are often cast off. But in God's eyes, a broken and a contrite heart is not despised but rather **required** for fellowship with Him.[1] Water always flows into the lowest places. We must see our own utter

---

1. Ps. 51:17; 69:29; 102:17; 113:7-8; 138:6; Matt. 5:3-5; 18:1-4; 20:25-28; 21:15-16; 23:10-12; Mic. 6:8; 1 Cor. 1:26-29

helplessness—the futility of all our own efforts; the insufficiency of our own strengths and abilities; the uselessness of all our mental exertions and intellectual endeavors; the failure of all our labors **apart from Him**.

God has chosen the foolish, weak, base and despised to show forth His glory and power. It is the proud and self-sufficient ones who are despised and brought down by God.[1] It is the weak and insufficient, the mere "earthen vessels", who alone are invited into His Presence. And they are invited there to **stay**.[2]

When we have come to the place of genuine heart-realization and acknowledgement that without Him we can do **nothing**, then we will be able for the first time to truly rely upon Him; and maintaining a constant vital contact with Him so that we can draw upon His inward supply of strength and power will be our only hope of a victorious life. We will become dependent upon Him—upon His continuous inward Presence and fellowship—for every need of every moment of every day. And this minute by minute union and communion is what He has promised us—if we will, in truth, give up our own life and strength, and instead choose His.

The Withdrawal of God's Presence

But in suggesting that there is a place of abiding fellowship with God promised to those who will walk in a life of complete and continuous surrender, we need to make some qualifications.

Firstly, we are not at all implying that there are never times when God deliberately withdraws His Presence from

---

1. Matt. 21:44; Jam. 4:6; Ps. 18:27; 138:6; Prov. 3:34; 1 Pet. 5:5
2. 1 Sam. 2:8; Is. 57:15; Ps. 34:18

146

His people. He **does** at times withdraw His comfort and inward fellowship from our lives, and the reasons for this are clearly given in Scripture:

> *Behold the LORD'S hand is not shortened, that it cannot save; neither His ear heavy, that it cannot hear:*
> *But your iniquities have separated between you and your God, and your sins have hid His face from you, that He will not hear.*
> *... The LORD is with you, while ye be with Him; and if ye seek Him, He will be found of you; but if ye forsake Him, He will forsake you. (Is. 59:1-2; 2 Chron. 15:2)[1]*

So we see that God, in chastisement, does withdraw His Presence in response to the sin and rebellion of His people. Should God do this to you—should He withdraw His Presence from you—this is **not** a trial to be endured. There is a **problem** with you. Something needs to be **changed** in you. **Repentance** is necessary for you to experience the restoration of God's Presence. At some point there is sin in your life or your heart. There is some sin of commission or omission. Maybe it is that you are not yielding to Him in an area He has spoken to you about.

This process of sin, the withdrawal of God's Presence in His chastisement, the repentance of His people and their return to God's favor and blessing, is beautifully described in the prophet Hosea:

---

1. see also Song of Sol. 5:2-6; Hos. 5:15; 10:12; Lam. 3:44; Ezek. 8:18; 1 Sam. 16:14; Gen. 3:24; Deut. 1:41-42; Ps. 51:11

I (God) will go and return to my place, till they acknowledge their offence, and seek my face: in their affliction they will seek me early.

Come (say the people), and let us return unto the LORD: for He hath torn, and He will heal us; He hath smitten, and He will bind us up ...

Then shall we know, if we follow on to know the LORD: His going forth is prepared (i.e. certain or sure) as the morning; and He shall come unto us as the rain, as the latter and former rain unto the earth. (Hos. 5:15-6:3)

Our second qualification is that we must allow for the times when God, in His sovereignty, may withdraw His manifest Presence from one whose heart is **right** with Him so that this one will faithfully and humbly commit his life to Christ in spite of dryness and unclearness, and thirst and cry after Him all the more. Thus our faith in God, which has been nourished during times of fellowship and communion with Him, will sustain us in spite of all difficulties and mysteries—including even the sovereign withdrawal of God's Presence. This sovereign withdrawal is infrequent, however, and the idea should not be used as an **excuse** for the general lack of God's Presence in the lives of His people.

The hidden darkness of our hearts and our own self-wills and stiff necks are far more often the cause of the loss of God's fellowship than His sovereign withdrawal. Furthermore, a sovereign withdrawal of God's Presence will only last for a season, until its perfect work is done; and then, like Job, the latter end of God's servant will be blessed more than his beginning.[1]

---

1. Job 42:12; Jam.5:11

God's Promise of Abiding Fellowship

One thing is certain: **irrespective of outward circumstances**, if you will draw near to God "He **will** draw nigh to you". Trials will not rob you of your inward fellowship with God. Trials **can** not rob you of your inward fellowship with God. The cry of the righteous is, "Thou, Lord, hast **not** forsaken them that seek thee". **Nothing** outside of ourselves "shall be able to separate us from the love of God, which is in Christ Jesus our Lord".

God has invited us to **dwell** in His secret place; to **abide** under His shadow; to make Him our **habitation**. "Son, thou art **ever** with me", is the inestimable privilege offered to us. "The Lord is **nigh** unto **all** them that call upon Him, to **all** that call upon Him in truth." "The upright shall **dwell** in (His) Presence." God is not denying Himself to you. "Him that cometh to me I will **in no wise** cast out." "Seek, and ye **shall** find". Those who hunger and thirst for God "**shall** be gorged (as a calf on clover)". "If any man hear my voice, and open the door, I **will** come in to him."[1]

There **is** a place of constant abiding in Him and He in you. Jesus, who told us to live by His life even as He lives by His Father's life,[2] lived constantly in the Presence of His Father—even in His greatest sufferings and trials. "He that sent me is with me: the Father hath not left me alone; for I do always those things that please Him." Thus the righteous are able to say to God: Thou "settest me before thy face (or Presence) for ever." "For the eyes of the Lord run to and fro throughout the whole earth, to shew Himself

---

1. Jam 4:8a; 2 Chron. 16:9; Ps. 9:10; Rom. 8:37-39; Ps. 91:1, 9; Luke 15:31; Ps. 145:18; 140:13b; John 6:37; Matt. 7:7; 5:6 (Williams trans.); Rev. 3:20

2. John 6:57

strong in the behalf of them whose heart is perfect toward Him."[1]

The danger of equating the loss of God's Presence with a trial of your faith is twofold. Firstly, if you are experiencing a loss of His fellowship in your life, this idea will allow you to rationalize that all is well with you and you simply need to endure this "trial" in your life, while in reality you need to be seeking God to find and deal with the reason for His withdrawal. Repentance is needed—self needs to be dealt with. But this is all avoided and a place of truth before God not achieved because you can tell yourself that you are all right and "it is just a trial". Thus you excuse the lack of the Presence of God in your life as a "trial", and self hides and earns a reprieve once again.

The second danger of this idea is that when you are experiencing a **genuine** trial of your faith you will likely not draw nearer to Jesus to receive His grace to enable you to overcome, because you can never be sure He will help you in this way anyway, and so you will seek to endure the trial in your own strength and power. As a result the purpose of the trial—namely that you lean upon Him more fully, and in His strength endure—is frustrated, and your maturity in God again checked.

But there **is** a place of constant abiding in Him. It is the place of obedience and abandonment. It is the place of yielding and surrender.

Hear the marvelous promise of Jesus:

> *He that hath my commandments, and keepeth them, he it is that loveth me: and he that loveth me shall be loved by my Father, and I **will love him, and will manifest myself to him**.*

---

1. John 8:29; 1 John 3:24; Ps. 15; 24:3-6; 41:12; 73:23-24; 148:14; Gen. 28:15; Ex. 33:14-16

Judas saith unto Him, not Iscariot, Lord, how is it that thou wilt manifest thyself unto us, and not unto the world?

*Jesus answered and said unto him, If a man love me, he will keep my words: and my Father will love him, and **we will come unto him, and make our abode with him.** (John 14:21-23)*

The Greek word that is translated "manifest" in these verses means "to physically and outwardly present one's self to the sight of another".[1] The word is used here to refer to an inward revelation of the Presence of Christ, and obviously the revelation is a very **real** one. It is not some abstract and judicial theory that is in view here, but a real experience of fellowship with God. This experience is not promised to anyone who merely identifies with Jesus or with His church, but only to those who truly love Him and obey Him. To those who will abandon all for Christ and surrender to Him entirely, this is a precious promise indeed: a promise of the **abiding** (that is, continuous) and **manifest** (that is, experienced) Presence and fellowship of God.

This experience of the Presence of God should not be confined to times of special prayer or church meetings, but it can be our daily and continuous possession. Jesus wants to make His **abode** with us. Moment by moment let us draw near to possess Him.

Some may recall how that God's Presence was so real and near to them when they were first saved, and yet since that time it has seemed like He has been far away and there is no real inward fellowship with Him in their lives. "Would not this mean that God is trying and testing me as I grow as a Christian?" one may ask. Far from it! It is

---

1. cf. verse 19 of the same chapter

151

more likely that **you** have left your first love, than that He has capriciously left you. "But," comes the reply, "when I was first saved there was much in my life that was wrong, and yet I knew the fellowship and Presence of God. Now I am obeying God so much more and yet lack His Presence. Surely this is simply a trial." Our answer to this is that as God gives us light and revelation of Truth, we must respond with obedience; and if we do not, then His Presence may be grieved away from us. It might be true that there is less sin in your life now than when you were first saved, but if you lack His Presence it means there are certainly some areas in which you are not yielding to Him.

What we are saying is that if you find yourself out of fellowship with God—out of inward communion with His Presence—then **STOP** and find the problem. Do not just go on and act like nothing is wrong. It is **not** just a trial of your faith. At some point you have left off walking in the light: "if we walk in the light ... we **have** fellowship one with another" (that is, with God).[1]

If you are out of fellowship with God that should distress you greatly. You should not be able to continue in that state. As Augustine said, "Thou hast made us for Thyself, and our souls are restless until they find their rest in Thee." Yield to the natural distress and restlessness within your soul when you find yourself away from Him, and seek restoration. Seek to find the problem and let fellowship be restored.

We are not suggesting that you are involved in some flagrant outward sin, but **at some point** you have left the light He has given you. As we grow in Christ, He gives us more and more light, and it takes less and less to grieve Him away. "Our vines have tender grapes". Maybe it was some inward thought of rebellion, bitterness, resentment or

---

1. 1 John 1:7

hatred, which to you seemed so unimportant, but to Him was so grievous. Maybe it was some unkind word to your neighbor. Perhaps He has revealed His will to you at some point, and you have not yet found it convenient or agreeable to obey Him. Perhaps your love for Him is not as intense as it should be. Perhaps you have taken His Presence for granted, as did the Shulamite, and have not responded as quickly as you should have to His gentle promptings and leadings for you to come apart for special seasons of love and communion with Him.[1]

But whatever it was, **let Him reveal the problem, repent, and let fellowship be restored.** Do not go on as if all was in order. If you continue on without God and His restraining Presence, "little" sins will grow into "bigger" ones, your heart will be progressively hardened, and it will become increasingly difficult for you to return to God.[2]

Genuine trials and tribulations should be joyfully endured, and their duration unquestioningly committed to your faithful Creator.[3] But the loss of the Presence of God in your life should not be endured any longer than the time it takes to fall to your knees, to seek His face that it may once again shine unobstructed upon your life. If you find yourself without Him, let your cry be:

> *Turn us again, O God, and cause thy face to shine ... (Ps. 80:3)*

Treat God's indwelling Presence with great concern. Treat His fellowship with great respect. Let nothing rob you of it. Do all you can to maintain it. Be jealous over

---

1. see Song of Sol. 5:2-6
2. Heb. 3:12-13
3. Jam. 1:2-4, 12; 1 Pet. 4:19; Ps. 105:19

it.[1] **God** is jealous over it: "the Spirit that dwelleth in us lusteth to envy".[2]

Do not go anywhere without God—without the inward consciousness of His fellowship. His Presence with you is what separates you from the rest of the world. Let your cry be, "If thy Presence go not with us, carry us not up hence."[3]

To walk in the light God gives you is to procure His abiding Presence; and continuing in His Presence is the wellspring of a life of faith and triumph.

Fellowship is Necessary for Faith

> *Beloved, if our heart condemn us not, then have we confidence toward God. And whatsoever we ask, we receive from Him, because we keep His commandments, and do those things that are pleasing in His sight.*
>
> *And he that keepeth His commandments dwelleth in Him, and He in him. And hereby we know that He abideth in us, by the Spirit which He hath given us. (1 John 3:21-22, 24)*

As the Apostle John says, when we obey God and walk in the light He gives us, His Presence—which we experience by His Spirit—is manifest to our lives. Because of this inward communion with Him, we have peace and assurance in our hearts, and confidence toward God that He will grant the requests we make of Him.[4]

---

1. Eph. 4:26a, 30
2. James 4:5b
3. Ex. 33:15-16
4. cf. John 15:7; 14:13-15

On the other hand, if we are out of fellowship with God, then we are **not** in a place where we can successfully pray the prayer of faith.[1] We must pray the prayer of repentance **first**, and then, when we are restored to communion and fellowship with God, can we have confidence toward Him. If there is sin in our hearts and we are out of fellowship with God, then He will **not** hear our prayer—no matter how many times we confess the promises and faithfulness of God.[2] It is only the true heart and the cleansed heart that can draw near to God to obtain His help in time of need.[3]

Here is the reason why many Christians pray what they think is a prayer of faith and yet fail to receive from God: because although they are out of fellowship with God they justify the loss of His Presence as being part of a trial or test, or they erroneously classify the inward consciousness of His fellowship as a "feeling" that is considered to be unimportant or even somehow opposed to "faith", and so they blithely try to obligate God to fulfill His promises **when they have not met the conditions**. But like Samson, when they shake themselves there is nothing there. God does not answer their prayers and they are frustrated, often becoming confused and doubting the validity or integrity of God and His holy promises.

But if we return to Jesus with broken and contrite hearts, abandoning all in surrender and obedience to Him, then we will know fellowship and communion with Him, and in times of trial and extremity His great power will be our resource.[4] Our times of weakness will become our times of greatest strength; because, releasing all hope and

---

1. see Ps. 66:18
2. Ps. 66:18
3. Heb. 10:22
4. 1 Pet. 1:5

trust in our own strength and in the things of this life to sustain us, we will throw ourselves more fully upon Jesus and His wonderful grace.[1]

If your relationship with God, however, is purely an abstract, mystical one; based entirely upon judicial doctrines and legal theories and principles; and it lacks reality, substance and vitality; then your only source of strength in times of suffering and testing will be yourself and your own religious will-power. By "religious will-power" we mean your own ardent zeal to make your life look like it all works, not only to others, but also to yourself and to God.

Does this portray you, dear brother or sister? Have we been describing your life all along? Do you really know the Presence of God in your heart? If you have known God and if you have experienced His Presence in the past, are you walking closely with Him today? Or have you left your first love, and are now following Him "afar off"?

Is your life characterized by a genuine fellowship of love for God and an experience of His fellowship and His love for you, or is there, as many say, "something missing"? Do you have a relationship with Jesus—a **real** relationship with Jesus—or is your spiritual life made up more of theory and "Christian philosophy" than of reality?

Is your life epitomized by these things: coldness toward God; indulgence toward yourself; the absence of self-giving love toward other men; criticism, jealousy, bitterness, censure, fault-finding and suspicion toward the brethren; a lack of anguish for the lost; little prayer outside of what is seen by others; a worship that is dictated more by the traditions and forms of men than by the outgushings of a heart captivated with Jesus; a greater interest in the

---

1. 2 Cor. 1:8-9; Ps. 20:7-8; 44:3, 5-7

things of this world than in the Word of God; a general apathy and boredom toward spiritual things in general?

Are rivers of living water flowing from your heart bringing healing and life to those who come in contact with you? Or is your life better described as "a well without water", or "clouds and wind without rain"? Do you possess **life** or merely "a name that thou livest"?

Do you see obedience, holiness and faith as privileges of your life or as duties? Are you more concerned that other Christians conform to your list of external religious forms than that they experience the inward substance and power of communion with Jesus? Are you irritated or made angry by what we have said in these chapters?

Does your Christianity consist more in make-believe than in real experience of God? Are you seeking to impress man while ignoring God, earnestly endeavoring to hide your spiritual boredom and to make your life appear exhilarating and successful lest all fail miserably, your grand religious edifice crumbling about your ears, and you exposed to those around you as a pretender?

Is your life being consumed in the exhausting pursuit of religious position, recognition and respectability; while all along neglecting the only One whose approval really matters, the only One who has any legitimate claim to your heart and life, the only One who can really set you free? Are you **truly** yielding to God from your heart day by day, or are you more preoccupied with outwardly appearing to men **as though** you do? Having begun in the Spirit, are you now made perfect by the flesh?

> *... thou sayest, I am rich, and increased with goods, and have need of nothing; and knowest not that thou art wretched, and miserable, and poor, and blind, and naked ... (Rev. 3:17)*

Oh, dear Christian, is there religious pretense in your life? If so, aren't you weary of it? Isn't the emptiness and destitution within beginning to disturb you? Isn't the selfishness and conceit of your life beginning to anger you? God's call to you is to be honest. Can you continue to lie about your true spiritual state to yourself, other men or God?

When He has offered you so much, how can you be content with so exceedingly little of God in your life?

Abandon this existence now and throw yourself upon the mercies of God, begging Him to make you real, pleading with Him to deal with your inner heart of hearts, imploring Him to change and enlarge your heart, bringing you to a place of honest and genuine submission to Him without which you can never know Him.

Tell Him you are tired of being a religious phony and that you want to know Him in truth. No longer will you be a man-pleaser and a lover of man's religion. No longer will you obey the orders of self, sin and Satan softly whispering that you serve them while maintaining an external religious facade of serving God. No longer will you deceive yourself that everything is all right when an aching void throbs within.

Jesus calls to you now:

> Behold, I stand at the door, and knock: if any man hear my voice, and open the door, I will come in to him, and will sup with him, and he with me.
> ... And let him that is athirst come. And whosoever will, let him take the water of life freely. (Rev. 3:20; 22:17)

Hear His voice! Open the door! Come! Take the Water of Life! Jesus offers Himself to you!

God has set eternity in your heart. Jesus has loved you with an everlasting love; therefore with lovingkindness is

158

He drawing you. No longer will you vainly try to be satisfied with what is less, so far less, so infinitely less than what He has offered you:

fully to enjoy Him forever!

Other Books Published by Pioneer Books

"In Him Was Life"
by Malcolm Webber

Christianity is man's enjoyment of God, and God's enjoyment of His man. And church life is corporate participation in the eternal fellowship of the Godhead. This book is about life: eternal life, the Christian life and corporate church life.

❧

"The Blood of God"
by Malcolm Webber

A systematic study of the Atonement of the Lord Jesus Christ. This book is comprehensive yet highly readable.

❧

"I Saw the Welsh Revival"
by David Matthews

A reprint of an eyewitness account of the outpouring of the Holy Spirit in Wales in 1904-05.

❧

"From the Plow Handle to the Pulpit"
by A.E. Humbard

A reprint of the famous life story of "Dad Humbard." Highly recommended!

❧